Growth, healing and peace (*shalom*) are inseparable parts of the same cluster. It is the cluster of discipleship which begins with grasping God's truth and ends with experiencing Christ's abundant life. Salvation is a rescue operation followed by progressive restoration into the image of Christ.

If you want to be helped in this divinely guided journey, read this book. *LifeCare* will show you how deep burdens from the past are not an obstacle, because, as the author says, 'relationships are formed and strengthened in the broken places – the "humble places" of spirit'. Solome Skaff has written a profoundly practical, biblical and enlightening book. It is my prayer that, as you read it, you may experience that change is possible because God is a specialist in restoring broken lives.

DR PABLO MARTINEZ
Psychiatrist, Author and Bible Teacher

The *LifeCare* course and book form a well-thought-through approach to emotional health and pastoral care. There are sound theological and psychological principles supported by the author's wide personal experience. The layout will encourage interaction and deeper learning. Complex issues are addressed safely and helpfully – with positive encouragement to seek relevant support alongside *LifeCare*. I recommend its use in churches and community groups who want to care for and grow people well.

DR ROB WALLER
Consultant Psychiatrist and Director of The Mind and Soul Foundation

D1493878

From who we are, and whose we are, to what we do and how we do it, this immensely practical and deeply theological book will take you on a journey to the heart of the matter. Whoever we are, and whatever we've done, we're known and loved by God. Practical exercises guide the reader to a new start, and personal stories of transformation offer glimpses of grace amidst the grit of real life. I would highly recommend *LifeCare* as a companion through the ups and downs we all will face.

REVEREND ALI HOGGER
Vicar, St Paul's Foleshill and Director of Keeping Health in Mind

LifeCare is an easy-to-use, practical approach to well-being and spiritual growth. Sol shares years of research and experience that just about anyone could use to build a healthy perspective on life and community. The material has been a blessing to me personally, and I've also found the content to be very effective in helping others. This is one of the best resources for personal growth in community that I've come across in my nine years as an organizational mission leader in Europe.

GREGORY L. NICHOLS, PHD
Regional Leader, Greater Europe Mission

How do we care well for the ninety-nine God has already sent us to shepherd, while also going out for lost sheep? *LifeCare* provides a model to not only manage that tension, but also provides a means to equip the saints for their work of ministry.

ANTHONY AND ZOE DELANEY
Ivy Church Network

I would highly recommend both the author and the content. Sol is a man of great integrity who has a passion for releasing potential in people. *LifeCare* is a thoughtful and empowering book and training that leads people to a place of freedom. It is a timely resource for us as a society with so many struggles, where people face change and uncertainty in culture, relationships and finances. This book will help them journey through the terrain of life in a more empowered, aware and purposeful way. Everyone is called to care, some are more natural than others, but this is a book that equips us all to become more fully human, while at the same time creating environments where people can flourish.

RICH ROBINSON
Founder & Leader of Catalyse Change, Director of 5Q Collective

There is hope here! No matter how stuck you feel, you can change. This book is not a prescription for an easy solution, nor a soothing tonic to deepen your denial. It's a guide to abundant life, and it will ask you to work. So if you are ready to grow, find in these pages a path towards redemption and the stories to prove you can get there.

AMY SIMPSON
Author of Troubled Minds: Mental Illness and the Church's Mission

LIFECARE

Published in 2019 by
Muddy Pearl, Edinburgh, Scotland.
www.muddypearl.com
books@muddypearl.com

British Library Cataloguing in Publication Data
A catalogue record for this book is available from the British Library

ISBN 978-1-910012-61-1

Typeset in Minion by Revo Creative Ltd, Lancaster, Lancashire
Cover design by Revo Creative Ltd, Lancaster, Lancashire
Cover image © Shutterstock 218365018 By Evannovostro
Illustration © Shutterstock 1008651205 By Ngukiaw, 228106534 By Atid28

Printed in Great Britain by Bell & Bain Ltd, Glasgow

LIFECARE

SOLOME SKAFF

Muddy
Pearl

CONTENTS

FOREWORD

'Do not expect us to visit you in your home'.

I actually said this as I interviewed for the job of pastor at my current church. (Niki, if she had been there, would have been appalled).

In the cold light of day and with the benefit of hindsight, it sounds like an unhelpful, arrogant statement and not the best way to get a job. But what I was trying to do was to communicate that my gifts lie elsewhere, and, more importantly, that the task of care in the body of Christ is a body ministry for *all* the body of Christ. Everyone gets to play and everyone *has* to play. The truth is, Niki and I are both pastors. We have to be, as leaders of God's people. The primary motif Jesus employs for himself is shepherd; The Good Shepherd, The Great Shepherd, *Poimen* …

So, whatever other significant gifts and callings you have in the body, you must care, emotionally, spiritually and physically. Care in the body of Christ is one of the significant testimonies that marks out his people from any other people.

'By this everyone will know that you are my disciples, if you love one another.'

JOHN 13:35 NIV

If we would care better, the world would see love better and know God better. It is for this reason that we have great delight in commending to you this book and this author. *LifeCare* will give you tools to know yourself, look after yourself, to know healing and freedom for yourself and to care well for the people that God has placed around you.

Both Niki and I have benefited personally from *LifeCare*. The profound honour of just being listened to well – with no judgment – is, in itself, life-changing. We have never been more aware of the dysfunction within our society and the brokenness of people as we are right now, yet the people of God have an opportunity to find themselves in the centre of God's repair job for this world. If you seriously engage with this book, you will be better for it, and so will others.

LifeCare is the real deal too. It is sophisticated enough to ask the right questions and accessible enough to offer real life solutions. Read it, do it, share it.

Karl and Niki Martin

PREFACE

Sometimes when we are hurt, or our goals are blocked, the veneer of our lives, the outer surface of image and position and routine, is pierced, cracked, creating a gap through which something meaningful might pass. A gap through which stories can be told and heard. Sometimes with these stories comes a lifting-up, a transformation, an emergence of purpose and vision.

My story is that, when I was a kid, I learned that coarse humour and rebellion got me more invitations to birthday parties and sleepovers. In high school I discovered various ways to escape boredom. Most of them were unhealthy, but their draw was inclusion in a counter-culture that provided community and identity.

At university I became a nihilist – that is, I believed in nothing. No meaning. No purpose. No God. I cringe to recall mercilessly teasing a girl at a party who had shared that she was a Christian, cackling with my friends as she burst into tears and ran out of the room. This kind of thing was, unfortunately, not uncommon. I didn't want to hurt her. I did want to ridicule the concept of God.

I thought of myself as strong and unafraid to face the stark truth about life. I thought of myself as a good person. A sign this was true, I thought, was that whenever I was around animals, they approached me without fear. Cats, dogs, birds … everything. I thought if there was a God, he too would have to acknowledge that I was good and let me in to heaven.

Then when I was twenty-two, my father developed a blood disease after minor surgery, went into a coma a few days later and died thirty-eight days after that. He was the hub of our family and social network, and with him gone, we all struggled and coped in our own ways – most of them unhealthy.

This period of my life reminds me of a town struck by a hurricane or tornado, everything tipped over and uprooted. Some things left standing next to others in nonsensical ways. A glass sitting calm, still, on a kitchen countertop whose wall has been ripped away, for example. Brittle blades of straw driven into a fence post like nails. You just look at it, tilt your head and wonder.

More than ever I wanted to lose myself – to be away from myself. To change the way I felt, thought, existed. In this state, I was wild. I hurt people with my choices. Some relationships endured, others were destroyed. Most were fundamentally changed.

It was then that I decided I could no longer believe that nothing mattered. And I no longer could believe that if there was a heaven, God would let me in. I'd created and broken my own 'law' by hurting others. And I had been hurt. My choices did matter – not just in a cause and effect sense, but in a way that was more profound. Choices, I discovered, are the mechanism we use to participate in the co-creation, or destruction, of the world.

Over time, these experiences prepared my heart in several ways. First of all, for marriage to a wonderful woman named Hillary, who began pointing me towards the Lord, and who has now been my wife for seventeen years and given me three beautiful children. Secondly, for a job at a community outreach charity in East Austin in 2002, led by just the right man to disciple me into a relationship with Jesus. When the charity was donated to a large suburban church, I transitioned along with it. An amazing opportunity to go to a seminary came and I took it, studying theology and counselling. Making up for lost time.

I had changed. And yet, my past was baked in to who I was in a way that would soon make itself felt in the form of anxiety at work.

I was given a pastoral position that required me, at times, to do some public speaking to the wider staff. Me, who just a few years earlier was breaking bottles over my head as a party trick and snowboarding behind cars on roads hard-packed with dirty snow, a sofa cushion duct-taped to my rear end for padding. Up until that time, I had only been called upon to speak and teach in the niche community of East Austin where I felt known and accepted. These were people whose lifestyles were familiar to me and I did fine there.

But most of the church staff had impressive qualifications, more wholesome backgrounds and had been following Jesus for decades. They couldn't have been more inviting, but because of my less than pure background, I felt I didn't belong. 'Imposter syndrome', some call it.

This revealed itself in a very tangible way whenever I was called upon to speak to them as a group. I would be OK for about thirty seconds, but, as the reality of the situation settled in, my mouth would go dry and my heart begin to race. My voice quivered and my breathing became shallow and unsteady. Then came the cold, relentless voice in my head:

'They see you sweating.'
'You don't know what you're doing.'
'What you've said is inaccurate and they all know it.'
'Everyone hears your voice shaking.'
'You don't belong here.'

Each thought flickered ghost-like through my synapses one after the next, each heightening the anxiety of the ones before it.

If I knew in advance that I would have to speak it was worse. I would struggle with anxiety whenever I thought about it for days ahead of the group meeting.

I tried to reason with my body, 'This is ridiculous, calm down!' I would tell it, 'There's nothing to be afraid of here! These are good people – they *like* you.' But my body simply would not listen. There seemed to be no way to stop these physiological reactions – they were coming from a place I had no control over.

I tried a number of things looking for a quick fix. Praying, distracting myself with other things right up until the time of my talk – I even tried biting my tongue or pinching myself hard to take my focus off the fact that I was going to have to speak. Nothing worked. I didn't understand it. I had never been afraid to speak publicly in the past. But I knew if I didn't figure it out, it would limit my potential.

At the same time, part of my new job was to start a recovery ministry at the church. As part of that process, I went through a systematic study of the 'twelve steps' in a group with about ten other men who were meant to be my first crop of leaders. I decided to do it with them to demonstrate solidarity. I didn't want to ask them to do something I wasn't willing to do myself. That was a good instinct. And yet, what is incomprehensible to me now, is that I thought the study really didn't have much to offer *me*.

Once we began, I found out how wrong I was. Right out of the gate, the questions challenged my willingness to share my experiences with others. I hung in there with the other men for a while. Then came steps four and five.

For the uninitiated, this is where you first catalogue all the things that others have done that hurt you, and all that you have ever done that hurt others. Then you share them with a sponsor. It feels a bit like one of those dermatology appointments where you have to completely disrobe and allow them to examine every square inch of your skin for odd looking moles, all while a nurse looks on in boredom for accountability purposes. In other words, it demands extreme vulnerability that you usually only undergo because you think it might save your life.

And it did. I don't know why I hadn't done anything like this sooner. God knows I needed it. But doing something healthy back then just never crossed my mind. Now here I was, and it was all coming out. I learned a lot through the process about myself and what made me tick. During this time, I processed my past extensively with God and others; made amends where I could; became willing to make amends if given the opportunity.

However, there were a few things I held back. I was ashamed of my past. And if I was going to talk about these things, I needed an even deeper level of confidentiality.

Meanwhile, my fear of public speaking wasn't going away.

Then, I had a dream. Not the Martin Luther King kind. Not really a nightmare either. Perhaps it was a vision. Whatever it was, it so impressed itself upon me that I wrote it down right after it happened. The two most significant aspects of it were that, at one point, some sort of demonic dog was chasing me and I was speeding away from it in a boat. It couldn't reach me, but it was pursuing me. I interpreted this as meaning that though the enemy could not separate me from the love of God, he still had me on the run.

Another significant aspect of the dream was a group of children from another land playing and leaping from tall cliffs into the water below. They were free and fearless. I wanted to join them, but I was afraid to leap from such great heights. I interpreted the leap they were making as representing the leap of faith it would take for me to trust someone enough to share the things I'd held back, allowing them to truly know me, with no guarantee of the outcome.

At the next meeting with my sponsor, I read my complete inventory list. I couldn't even look up at him as I spoke. I braced for his shock, rejection or condemnation. Instead, he only seemed to love me more. He reassured me. He told me that he respected my honesty and put some of my fears to rest with his kind words. I had known of God's grace, but this was an experience of it. It came from God, through my sponsor, to me directly in a way that I could see, hear and touch.

It was then that I began thinking that if a person could feel this way about me, knowing everything about me, then maybe God could too. Slowly, I began believing that maybe Jesus really did forgive and love me unconditionally, just as he said he did in his word. Maybe I really did have value, regardless of my mistakes.

It was about this time that my fear of public speaking started to melt away. I could speak, catch my breath and no longer tremble when I spoke.

My participation in recovery continued along with my training in theology, counselling and coaching. I stacked up new skills and techniques on top of my newfound confidence. I learned to monitor and capture destructive or distorted thoughts and replace them with new ways of thinking that were more consistent with my most deeply held convictions and goals. I learned how to regulate my emotions and developed a handful of tools that worked best for me. I developed new relational tools. My wife joined me on this journey, leading alongside me in the recovery and coaching ministry, allowing God to work in and through her as well.

Speaking for myself, I want to be clear that when I have problems, though I often know what to do, and how to do it, I still don't do it. That's because I still contend with my flesh – my desire to do what I know is wrong or hurtful. To follow my impulses in a thoughtless way. Sometimes I make good choices and sometimes I don't. I don't envisage that ever changing, but I'm a lot further down the road of spiritual and emotional health than I once was. And when I do fail, my recovery time is a lot quicker. My faith is not in my skills, nor is it any longer in my innate 'goodness' or what others think about me. Instead, it is in the everlasting, unchanging grace of God who is always waiting on the horizon to run to me, even when I've been selfishly squandering his riches.

One of the exciting things he's done in my life is to give my family and me this ministry, which is a way to care for and coach others out of our own brokenness. We're grateful for the opportunity to have done this in pastoral ministry in the US, the UK and Europe, and I can tell you that people all over the world need the same thing – an accessible space to process life events with someone they trust, who can help them work through adversity, heal, develop solutions and build a vision of the good life. Someone who can help them move forward, based on a solid foundation.

And that is what this book is. Ecclesiastes 1:9 tells us that there is nothing new under the sun, and I believe that. Still, these ideas and methods may be new to you, or perhaps just presented in a way that clicks for you. My hope and prayer is that our wonderful Lord, Jesus, will minister to you in a deep and lasting way through them as he has done and continues to do for me.

God bless you

Sol

HOW TO USE THIS BOOK

Blessed are they who see beautiful things in humble places where other people see nothing.

CAMILLE PISSARRO, IMPRESSIONIST PAINTER

The world breaks everyone and afterward many are strong at the broken places. But those that will not break it kills. It kills the very good and the very gentle and the very brave impartially. If you are none of these you can be sure it will kill you too but there will be no special hurry.

ERNEST HEMINGWAY, *A FAREWELL TO ARMS*

WE WERE NOT MADE TO GO IT ALONE

It's not just you. Other people struggle too, and with all kinds of things. Workplace challenges, periods of depression, anxious thoughts, feelings of hopelessness, anger, regret, loss, relationship trouble, uncertainty about life, temptation, secrets, spiritual questions. These are a normal part of the human experience.

But there is hope. In this life people overcome obstacles and make progress, bored people find joy, stuck people are set free, purpose and meaning are found, people enslaved to addiction find sobriety, hearts wracked with guilt find forgiveness and those overcome with shame find acceptance and redemption.

This study will help you begin that process in your own life, ushering you beyond mere existence towards a vision of the life you were created to live. You can get there. The first step is the decision to actually begin the journey.

Often, as people work through these struggles, they gain a capacity for self-insight and compassion that transforms them into effective carers and healthy leaders. Skills can be taught. But people who face adversity with another alongside them gain qualities that cannot be taught.

The alternative is to attempt to isolate and face your challenges alone. This is not a healthy choice. The Bible says it this way, 'Pride goes before destruction, and a haughty spirit before a fall' (Proverbs 16:18). The most competent, functional people find value in transparent relationships, know themselves and put themselves in a position to receive feedback from others so that they can gain self-awareness, grow from their mistakes, be encouraged and capitalize on their successes.[1]

Later in this book, we will introduce you to several wonderful, loving people who have been through the LifeCare course and served as carers for others. It is a course which encourages sharing and connection with others. A social laboratory where people learn skills to help others, and in the process learn what it is like to receive help, set goals and forge meaning.

Relationships are formed and strengthened in the broken places – the 'humble places' of spirit, similar to the 'humble places' of life that Pissarro alluded to. Connection with God, and one or two others that you can really trust, often starts in the cracks, in the humble breaking. Not in stale, boring acquaintance where appearances are maintained. Once the facade is chipped and fractured there's no point in that anymore. Instead, vibrant, real relationships can develop, where people are saying what they actually think and feel rather than what they think will sound good to others on social media, or during a brief chat over coffee at church.

1 Thomas Maeder, 'Wounded Healers' in *The Atlantic*, Vol. 263(1) (1989), p.37. The 'helping professions,' notably psychotherapy and the ministry, appear to attract more than their share of the emotionally unstable.

This way of relating to God and others can give you the confidence to change the way you relate to people in general. It can change the way you relate to the events of your life, and the way you think about your future and purpose. As you change you may find some comfort in spite of whatever you've lost, as your outside gets closer and closer to matching your inside. Psychotherapists call this 'congruence'. Jesus calls it the truth that sets you free. You might even sense yourself gaining a new compassion for others that is fuelled by the compassion that has been offered to you.

GETTING STARTED

This book will get you started, or perhaps encourage you to continue on in your process. Please don't put it down. Because actually, we need you. We need the strength you will find through your weakness, and the love that you will pour out to others once you have been filled with it yourself. We need the passion you'll bring to leading and caring for others because you've been the one in need of a bit of care yourself at some point.

STORIES

For five wonderful years of ministry, my wife and I led, and participated in, a Christian discipleship ministry called Celebrate Recovery.[2] Most of the stories told by the people in this book were part of that ministry. They entered hurting and seeking help, and God began working in them. Not long after, he also began working *through* them. They served in the recovery ministry, and then as part of their ongoing development and service later went through LifeCare, did some further processing and learned new tools that would help them care for and coach others.

Bonnie's experience, below, shows what incredible self-insight and strength can be found by opening up about the difficult things you've survived, and the way these incidents have affected you:

2 For more information on this Christ-centred, twelve-step programme, see their website https://www.celebraterecovery.com.

Bonnie

When I first wrote out my history and shared it with the person who was leading me through this process, it was the first time I had ever shared about my mother shaking me and it was the first time I had someone view this as child abuse. I was able to see the effects this had on me so early on in my life, forgive my mother's rants and thank God that I lived through all that. I also was able to see how I craved attention and made things so much worse by lying, stealing, controlling and escaping to survive or keep out of trouble. I saw each person's faults in order to forgive them, but I really became aware of my own actions too. I realized that I used the limited tools that I had at my disposal as a child, and they helped me to survive in some ways, but now that I was an adult these same tools don't work anymore. As an adult, there are now new tools that are available to me, and I am learning what they are and how to use them.

For example, I asked forgiveness from my husband for my controlling behaviour. I asked him for forgiveness for always having my own agenda. I confessed that I certainly did not know how to be a father (I used to tell him how a man ought to do this), and that I was even unsure of the right way to mother our two boys, especially now that they are adults. My husband loves me and graciously forgives me.

I confronted my son for hurting me by the destructive choices he is making. He is responsible for those choices and I can't take them personally. I have recognized that God has him in a process like he did me. I am free to love him and pray for him along the way.

My husband and I are better now, and I have no shame, no guilt and I experience joy and peace often.

YOUR STORY

Don't make the mistake of thinking that you have nothing to learn from someone like Bonnie – who by the way is such a fun, kind and lively person, as is every one of the people you will hear from as we go along. If you met them, you would never guess the things they've been through; though you wouldn't have to because they would freely share their story with you if you asked. But the principles they worked through as they developed are all rooted in Scripture. The people who contributed their stories to this book have grappled with elements of discipleship that may be easy enough to learn in theory, but challenge and transform hearts and lives when applied with purpose.

You, too, have a story to tell. You may or may not consider it to be dramatic, but that isn't the point. It's your life, your experience, your feelings, your thoughts and your future that count. This is about your goals, your challenges. The material ahead will help you to tell your story and learn from it.

This book is rooted in Scripture, but also draws from social theory, counselling and psychotherapy research, time-tested discipleship and life-coaching practices and the experiences of LifeCare training participants.

We will hear from various writers and spiritual leaders, and even get a bit of exposure to the work of some of the leading writers on the implications of quantum theory to the social world. By the end of this journey we will have been given a blend of practical tools and techniques that are biblically based and research validated. We will explore God's word together, and there will be the opportunity for you to think about your own life and write down your thoughts.

ACTIVE PARTICIPATION

Please be warned! Just reading on its own won't help, I'm sorry to say. It would be easier if it did. But it doesn't. I've just never seen it work that way – for me, or anyone. Lasting change will come only as you open yourself up to new experiences and new ways of thinking and relating.

You have to read, you have to think, you have to write. Please don't skip the 'Reflect and Write' sections. This whole process just doesn't work without them.

Perhaps you are coming to this material feeling a bit cracked or broken yourself. You're looking for answers, ready to stop trying to change things your way and have become willing to give it a try God's way. Or you may be feeling pretty good and just wanting to learn how to help others. This material will help you in either case, but it is essential that you be willing to explore the difficult things in your life before you put yourself in a position to help others.

Stop. Breathe. You don't have to do it all at once.

TIME AND SPACE FOR THINKING

This book is a great way to get started because it affords you safe, private, non-judgmental, confidential exposure to ideas and principles that may be new to you. It gives you space to think and write about them. This is good. God made the world and people in such a way that we need input from one another for our psychological well-being. Neuropsychologist Dr Curt Thompson writes:

> *You cannot know God if you do not experience being known by him. The degree to which you know God is directly related to your experience of being known by him. And the degree that you are known by him will be reflected in the way in which you are known by other people.*

*In other words, your relationship with God is a direct
reflection of the depth of your relationship with others.*[3]

This may be one of the reasons the Bible is filled with 'one anothers'
(love one another, encourage one another, bear one another's
burdens, etc.). It may also be why the dominant metaphor for the
Church is the body of Christ – all the different parts connecting
together to do something they could never do alone.

CHANGE IS POSSIBLE!

Time and time again, people who were lost become found. Goals
are reached. Challenges overcome. Vision realized. Suffering acts
as a catalyst for connection, and through connection comes a life
with heart.

You, too, can find these things and more. The change is
already beginning as you invest time in reading this book, which
itself is like a little mechanism built of letters doing its work in
your soul, heart and mind.

As life keeps coming – as new problems arise and old
challenges resurface – you can try to ignore them, as you may
have done in the past; but as you well know by now, they will
continue regardless. The past impinges on the present as though
it snuck through a hole in space-time, blinking into your life.
You can, instead, choose to harness these entanglements. To not
become victim to them. To allow yourself to be unmade and
made again, trusting in who you are and the One who loves you
to guide you into something that, in the end, I must believe by
faith, will be worth the struggle. Something that might even be
beautiful.

3 Dr Curt Thompson, *Anatomy of the Soul: Surprising Connections between Neuroscience and Spiritual Practices that
can Transform your Life and Relationships* (Tyndale, 2010), p.24.

CHAPTER 1

CONNECTIVITY

Events in your own life have shaped you, whether it is simply being lost as a child in a supermarket, or whether you suffered a serious accident. You are not an isolated entity, choosing what you will or will not let in. Even if something happened and you decided never to speak of it or think about it again, and even if you did everything you could to forget about it, those decisions to close up a part of yourself are themselves the impact of those events. Those decisions have shaped you.

It is neither bad nor wrong to set some things aside. It may be necessary at times for survival, even for growth. Yet those events are still in there, somewhere, affecting you somehow. That's just how it works. Understanding that they happened, the effect they had upon you, then choosing to set them aside is different from pretending they never happened and just moving on. Try though you might, there is no way to stand outside of, exterior to, the events of your life.

LIKE EGGS IN A CAKE

You personally may not be able to relate to the following story. The things he describes may seem completely foreign to you or they may sound hauntingly familiar. But I have chosen to begin with Malik's story because it is a great example of what it looks like for someone to be aware of where they have been, understand what it is that matters about it, and move forward.

Malik

I have had two lowest points that resulted in change. Before I discuss the actual two lowest points of my life, I want to highlight a few points that were not my lowest points:

- *Totalling my 1969 Mustang, 1990 Lumina and 1979 280ZX whilst intoxicated.*
- *Getting into three motorcycle crashes.*
- *Urinating on myself whilst passed out in the car in front of my parent's house, with my head on the steering wheel, honking the horn.*
- *Passing out in my car and in clubs.*
- *Getting a ticket for driving whilst intoxicated.*
- *Spending large amounts of money to feed my addictions.*
- *Getting fired from my first engineering job.*
- *Getting caught in behaviour related to my sexual addiction.*
- *Smoking so much marijuana that it put me in the hospital because of my asthma.*
- *Saying 'yes' when I meant 'no' so many times because of my co-dependency.*

Those are a few things that come to mind when thinking about low points, but they are not my lowest points ...

Malik did what he could to move on, to leave these events behind him and not to think about them. But they were in him, layered into him and constituting him, like eggs in a cake. They had a profound effect, contributing to decisions he would make later, which you will read about in the pages ahead. And now, he uses his experience in the form of testimony, motivation for service to others and ongoing personal growth.

THE BIG PICTURE

Our connections are not always simple and straightforward. They are entangled and complex and we will never fully understand the big picture until God chooses to show it to us. There are a couple of levels to this.

The Butterfly Effect

In the 1970s, Edward Lorenz studied the complexity of weather patterns. He discovered that if you change even the smallest factor in a weather system, it has a massive knock-on effect which leads to huge changes to the system down the line. He called his paper 'Predictability: Does the Flap of a Butterfly's Wings in Brazil Set Off a Tornado in Texas?'. Later, a film entitled *The Butterfly Effect*[4] led to the theory entering popular consciousness. The idea that seemingly insignificant factors can lead to life-changing effects is not new. A proverb dating back to at least the thirteenth century plays with similar themes:

> *For want of a nail the shoe was lost.*
> *For want of a shoe the horse was lost.*
> *For want of a horse the rider was lost.*
> *For want of a rider the message was lost.*
> *For want of a message the battle was lost.*
> *For want of a battle the kingdom was lost.*
> *And all for the want of a horseshoe nail.*

AUTHOR UNKNOWN

Lorenz's point, however, was that it's not as straightforward as that. When a big change in a weather system (or in a life) develops, it is very difficult to determine what factors caused them. Each change, each cause and effect, creates new conditions that create new conditions, and so on, until looking back the pattern

4 Eric Bress, J. Mackye Gruber, *The Butterfly Effect* FilmEngine; BenderSpink; Katalyst: (2004).

is hopelessly entangled. Every change is the culmination of thousands of other untraceable, seemingly unconnected changes.

What does this mean to a life? To a momentous decision? To a life-altering consequence?

You were born into this cause and effect system. And it has been going on since Adam and Eve, perhaps before. It is a system that determines certain parameters within you which have the ability to make decisions. There were parameters around your opportunity for education, your ethnicity and society which you could not change, the privilege or disadvantage that you were born into, your access to faith, the provision or resources you had access to, and more.

These parameters mattered a great deal. And so did your response to them. You could spend a lot of time just thinking about the parameters that influenced what you did or didn't do in life, what seemed in reach, or impossible or never even occurred to you.

The Quantum Level

The second level of connection we need to briefly explore is the quantum (which means the smallest amount possible) level. Don't be scared by that term. We won't get into it too much, but to skip over it is to miss something profound in the general revelation of God's existence. Consider the following:

> There is no discrete 'I' that precedes its actions. Our (intra) actions matter – each one reconfigures the world in its becoming – and yet they never leave us; they are sedimented into our becoming, they become us. And yet even in our becoming there is no 'I' separate from the intra-active becoming of the world. Causality is an entangled affair ...

KAREN BARAD[5]

You hear a lot of talk about how quantum mechanics says

---

5 Karen Barad, *Meeting the Universe Halfway: Quantum Physics and the Entanglement of Matter and Meaning,* (Duke University Press, 2007), p.394.

everything is all interconnected. Well, that's not quite right. It's more than that; it's deeper. It's that those connections, your connections to all the things around you, literally define who you are, and that's the profound weirdness of quantum mechanics.

AARON O'CONNELL[6]

You might want to re-read those a couple of times. There's a lot there.

At both the quantum and social levels, we are not isolated from the world around us; in fact, the opposite is true. Every interaction we have, in our thoughts, with people, with the material world around us – both biological and non – has profound implications.

Included in this connective mix is God the Potter, working the clay, before, over and above it all:

Yet, LORD, you are our father.
We are the clay, and you are our potter;
we are all the product of your labor.

ISAIAH 64:8

In what sense are we clay? In what sense does he shape us? The answer is that God is working to shape and mould us into the image of his Son. One way he does this is by working through our connectedness to one another and to the physical world around us. This adds weight to the 'one anothers' of Scripture, which are meant to be the operating instructions for The Body – how we are meant to relate, connect and build one another up. But of course, it doesn't always work that way. Because there is an enemy who wants the clay to wobble, wants to thin the walls of the vessel and see it collapse. But our Potter is skilled and faithful. He knows how to deal with this interference to his craftsmanship and reclaim the vessel.

---

6 Aaron O'Connell, 'Making sense of a visible quantum object', TED (June 2011), https://www.ted.com/talks/aaron_o_connell_making_sense_of_a_visible_quantum_object.

Birdie's story illustrates this point:

Birdie

It has now been twenty-two years since I was stalked and attacked, since I was abandoned by my friends and community in high school (nearly to the day as I write this). I can't fully grasp how, but I know it's significant, and that God is using it right now. I know that God does not waste anything in our lives – not one single hurt, habit or hang-up. Just as he redeemed my life from the grave when I turned to him in faith, he is redeeming my every day, my every struggle. Five years after entering recovery I now get to recruit and raise up female leaders, train and shepherd women as they lead in their small groups, and occasionally teach. I also sponsor a precious woman named Mary, and I get to see Jesus show up in her life and recovery time and time again. God has blessed me so abundantly through her. In addition to all this, Jesus is loving me incredibly well through many other women. I had such trauma, fear and dislike of people in the past; and now God is giving me new experiences to redeem my past. One of the ways he is healing me is through people.

Birdie's past connections and experiences led to isolation and feelings of abandonment. Then she formed new connections. Materially. Physically.

She took a courageous step. She allowed light to slip through the cracks – in a gracious church environment that supported her and encouraged outreach through care ministries. These new connections, little by little, changed not only her perspective, but her material reality. Her choices.

Over time those traumatic connections of the past that used to hold her back became the driving force behind her passion to love and care for others. It is not that the events of her past changed. She changed the way she viewed her past, which changed what she did with it materially in her present; where she went, the stories she told, the emotions she felt, the way she related to God about it, the people she entered into relationship with and why.

This is more than just 're-framing the past', as if the past were an isolated object on a dusty dark shelf awaiting manipulation. Instead, this is Birdie forming new connections in the present that become the fingers and palms of the Potter on her life. Allowing new words to be spoken over her, new ways of viewing the past to be suggested, new opportunities to transform her future and that of those around her.

GOD'S WORK

> ... *at the quantum level, there is, in Polkinghorn's phrase 'togetherness in separation'. This is unexpected and unexplained and yet is part of the way the world is. It may indicate that relationality is a fruitful way of thinking more about God's interaction with the universe ... In terms of personal salvation, God is active before conversion, during conversion, and in the growth to holiness. God is active in both preparing this path and in helping along the way.*

DAVID WILKINSON[7]

Knowing how God has worked in the past, and how he has moulded us, informs our decisions about what to do in the present.

It is important to remember that God is not just an idea. He is an actual being who does things in the world. He created, out of nothing, everything that is (Genesis 1:1–2). I am not saying that he created the mix then stepped away from it and let the chain reactions ensue. He created the mix, is in the mix and is stirring the pot all at the same time. His influence has been present from

7 David Wilkinson, *When I Pray What Does God Do?* (Monarch Books, 2015), pp.154, 179.

the start and has been layered into everything that has followed and will be to come.

His very essence is connective, as he himself is three-in-one. He is relational entanglement personified. You see his triune nature reflected in passages like, 'In the beginning was the Word, and the Word was with God, and the Word was fully God' (John 1:1), and, 'Now the Lord is the Spirit, and where the Spirit of the Lord is present, there is freedom' (2 Corinthians 3:17).

Word (Jesus), Spirit, Father – distinct but connected in himself. It is no wonder, that just as man was created to be relational in his image, so too the rest of creation has been shaped and moulded to be relationally intra-active with itself and with God.

> ... *for all things in heaven and on earth were created in him – all things, whether visible or invisible, whether thrones or dominions, whether principalities or powers – all things were created through him and for him. He himself is before all things and all things are held together in him.*

COLOSSIANS 1:16-17

Scripture tells us exactly what we ourselves are, and that is an intra-active mix of earth and Spirit:

> *The LORD God formed the man from the soil of the ground and breathed into his nostrils the breath of life, and the man became a living being.*

GENESIS 2:7

When we die, we will return to the earth and our spirit will return to our Creator:

> *So remember your Creator in the days of your youth – before ... the dust returns to the earth as it was, and the life's breath returns to God who gave it.*

ECCLESIASTES 12:1,7

Our profound connectedness also enabled Jesus to make a sacrifice that became available to pay the debt of sin for every man, woman and child who came before or after him, if they just believed (Romans 5:15–21; John 5:24, John 11:25–26, John14:12).

What is Belief?

At least in some ways, belief is a decision to accept, or to receive, an assertion of truth about how all creation, our existence, our purpose all fit together.

In this case, it is the acceptance of his offer for connection with the very centre of your being, otherwise known in the Scriptures as your heart. Keep that possibility in mind, and this concept of one thing being layered *into* another, relationally and materially connected within in the present moment, as you read the following verses:

> 'You will know at that time that I am in my Father and you are in me and I am in you.'

JOHN 14:20

> 'I am the vine; you are the branches. The one who remains in me – and I in him – bears much fruit, because apart from me you can accomplish nothing … Just as the Father has loved me, I have also loved you; remain in my love. If you obey my commandments, you will remain in my love, just as I have obeyed my Father's commandments and remain in his love.'

JOHN 15:5, 9–10

> 'I have told you these things so that in me you may have peace.'

JOHN 16:33

For from him and through him and to him are all things.

ROMANS 11:36

And he himself gave some as apostles, some as prophets, some as evangelists, and some as pastors and teachers, to equip the saints for the work of ministry, that is, to build up the body of Christ, until we all attain to the unity of the faith and of the knowledge of the Son of God – a mature person, attaining to the measure of Christ's full stature. ... From him the whole body grows, fitted and held together through every supporting ligament. As each one does its part, the body grows in love.

EPHESIANS 4:11–13, 16

Our connection is not something that developed by chance. We are connected because we were created for connection, by a God whose very essence is connectivity. And not just us, but the universe around us. Through that connectivity comes the ability, and the responsibility, to love one another well so that we might build up the whole body of Christ into the full image of Christ.

But all connected systems have a vulnerability. If a virus gets in, it can wreak havoc. And it has. And it does.

THE VIRUS IN THE SYSTEM

Our connectivity gives us a way to think about *how* the enemy has attacked. It is a brilliant attack by a formidable opponent. Understanding the connective nature of the universe, the enemy knew that all he had to do was slip a virus into the system, and that once in, it would spread throughout the whole. That virus is sin. It was not a butterfly's wing, but the flicker of a serpent's tongue in the Garden of Eden that was enough to infect creation.

He knew that the sins of the first man and woman could not, would not be contained (Genesis 3:14–24) within the universe as

God created it. He knew that their sin, once committed, would radically alter the trajectory of all creation, and every man, woman and child that came after them (Romans 5:12, 17a). The adversary knew that our connectedness meant that the sins of the father would travel down through the generations (Exodus 20:5). It was inevitable, because those actions of past generations would come to constitute the world successive generations would be born into, limiting or enabling them to act.

At the same time, the enemy wants to convince us that we are not connected. He wants us to feel as though we are alone, disconnected, worthless and hopeless. He wants to create the illusion that we are isolated. Out of reach. That it is too late for help, or change or grace.

Our hope lies in the fact that we are not alone. That God is constantly shaping us through one another. That our acceptance of and connection to his truth is always just one decision away.

And yet our connectivity is also our greatest vulnerability, because through it, the destructive lies of the enemy influence us and the generations we follow or precede.

THE WAY FORWARD

It is for these biblical, social and material reasons that we will attend not only to present relationships, but also to past and future relationships. We will attend to our history. Not to cast blame but to gain insight into who we are, what our values are and how we got them. Not to wallow, but to gain compassion for ourselves, and perhaps for others, and understand how we got to where we are today.

We are response-able, and so we are responsible for what we choose, and for what we do not choose. What we enable is as important as what we constrain. I wonder if this principle has anything to do with the somewhat cryptic, oft debated meaning of Jesus' comment to Peter:

Truly I tell you the truth, whatever you bind on earth will be bound in heaven, and whatever you loose on earth will be loosed in heaven.

MATTHEW 18:18 NIV

In any case, we need to understand the way we think. About who we are. What we are. Our purpose. What we have been taught about ourselves. What we agree with and what we don't. What is helpful and what is not in becoming who we feel called to become. Because those thoughts are swirling around in our choices too.

That is why we do this together. Because contrary to what the enemy would have us believe, in this life at least, there is no apart.

Not from one another, and not from the God who loves us, died for us, gave himself for us and gave us to one another as allies in this life. We can wash ourselves in him. We can avail ourselves of his offer of reconciliation, put our faith in his word and begin to allow his Spirit to transform our heart and work its way out into our bodies, transforming our minds and actions, spilling out through our mouths, hands and feet into the world around us.

It is up to us whether we step into those relationships, take on those entanglements, become willing to go to war with the lies, make room for the redemption of our past and become who we were created to be.

It'll be messy, joyful and also likely to be painful at times. Yet it is often at the point of pain – the limits of what you think you can handle – that new growth begins and you discover you were created in a way that is far more magnificent than anything you had imagined.

SEEING YOURSELF IN YOUR WRITING.

Throughout this book, you will find questions to help you begin to apply the material you read. It is up to you whether you take the time to reflect and write. However, research does suggest that we connect to different parts of ourselves when we write. As we move the pen, fragments seem to come together in new ways. Therefore, to consolidate your learning, don't rush through the material. Take your time and do the journalling as you go along.

WRITE AND REFLECT

What do you think about the idea that who and what you are today has been influenced by the context into which you were born and raised?

How do you feel about the prospect of taking a closer look at those influences?

If you feel resistant to such an exercise, where does that resistance come from?

CHAPTER 2

WHAT MAKES YOU VALUABLE

Mike

I am a grateful believer in Jesus Christ and I struggle with alcohol, drugs, money, sex, religion and anything else that changes the way I feel. I identify myself as a believer in Christ. That is where my identity lies. I think that is a very important distinction. That's also an important part of my story. My identity, or who I think I am inside, and who I want you guys to think I am has a lot to do with my struggles and how I deal with them. I used to be, and still am to some degree, very good at wearing masks.

WHO YOU ARE, AND WHAT YOU ARE

Since I am encouraging you to dig deep in the pages ahead, I want to make sure that you are firmly rooted in who and what you are, and where you derive your sense of purpose and value. This is the strength you need to weather the storms of life.

For that reason, I want to ask who and what you are in the core of your being? Do you know the difference between the question of who you are versus what you are?

Who you are

There are parts of you which will change and develop during your life – that is your 'identity'. Your identity answers the question, 'Who am I?' Your identity is often not just how you see yourself, but also how the world sees you.

The concept of 'identity' includes things like roles, such as mother or engineer or writer, but it can also include certain personality traits, like whether you are talkative or shy, sporty or intellectual. An identity is something that does become a significant part of us and is layered into us once we take it on. For example, once you become a husband or wife, a mother or father, or achieve something significant, you are changed in a way that becomes material. You will change the way you think about yourself, yes, but you will also change your social circle, where you go or don't go, what you do or don't do. Your identity is a big deal.

And if, for example, you were to get divorced or your relationship with your child changed, or you made some sort of public mistake that damaged your reputation, then it is possible that these identities would change. You might not consider yourself a father, or wife or a member of your profession, anymore. You might begin identifying yourself with your mistakes or the tragedies that have befallen you – and other people might start identifying you with them too – especially if they are public. Resilient though you may be, these changes would probably be very painful, and will be sedimented into you, as the ongoing effects of the happenings and decisions of that phase of your life play out in the present.

The same can be true of other roles that change naturally over the course of time, or which a person chooses to leave behind. Whether chosen or inevitable, it can still be quite difficult. We have all experienced this in one way or another. Our role at a company ends, or shifts, and we no longer hold the same title or order our day around those responsibilities. Though that time in our lives affected and shaped us, we don't identify ourselves by that title or role anymore, nor do others and, though it is hard, it is time to move on. At best, you leave behind a positive legacy that contributes to your ongoing influence in the world in some new capacity. At worst, you are replaced and forgotten.

There is, of course, an identity that you can acquire that you can never lose. But we'll talk about that more later.

What you are

However, what you are at your very core is not something you can step into or out of. 'What' you are implies some sort of materiality. The image of God is in you because there was a point in time when God, a real being, made you that way; Scripture says he knit you together in your mother's womb (Psalm 139:13). James, the brother of Jesus, affirms in the New Testament period that we still carry God's image in us (James 3:9). This is true whether you or others know it or not, accept or reject it, or tend to drift away from your understanding of it. It is just simply in you, like DNA, affecting you deeply, wherever you go, whatever you do, regardless of what you think or believe about it.

That said, your understanding (or lack thereof) of what you are in the present moment will, in a significant way, affect what you come to believe about who you are, and therefore will affect the way you think and feel, and the things you choose to do or not do, and your experience of this life in general. Your understanding will shape what you become – what you do with what you are.

Take a hammer, for instance, made of wood and metal. If I look at it as a tool, which is what it was meant to be, I can pound nails with it. If instead I look at it as a weapon, or a boomerang, or a paperweight or a work of art, I am likely to do other sorts of things with it. The hammer is still what it is – wood and metal fitted together in a particular shape. But how I use it, and the impact it makes in the world, depends on what I think it is – within limits, of course. It will never be a glass of water, or a jar of peanut butter or a living giraffe. What we make of it is restricted by what it is in a material sense.

It's the same with you. What you are – made in God's image and worth enough to die for – doesn't change and you simply don't have any choice in the matter. Like the prodigal son (Luke 15) you can run from the Father, but no matter how far you go. or what you do, you are still made in his image, shaped in a particular way, and he will always be waiting for you when you decide to come home. But the way you interact with what you are can and does change, and does make a difference in you and the world around you. It is not up to you to decide what you are. It is up to you to decide what to do with what you are.

For that reason, what you understand to be true about what you are in the deepest foundation of your being is important to the work ahead. If you are deceived about it, it will be your greatest vulnerability as this deception shapes the way you think about who you are. On the other hand, if you clearly understand what you are, it will provide you with a never-ending source of rest, value and hope – even in the midst of challenge. When your understanding of what you are lines up with your understanding of who you are, you grow deep roots that become cemented into an eternal foundation (see Jeremiah's Tree in Chapter 7). And from that foundation, you can move forward with confidence, knowing that even when all else fails, as identities you take on or have thrust upon you come and go, you will not be uprooted. The foundation will not shift or change but will hold you fast. And from that place of strength, you can plot a way forward and forge a new identity, new roles and relationships, once again.

In the pages ahead, I'll tell you more about what God's authoritative and reliable word says you are. It is not just true because we believe it. It is not a psychological trick, a concept or an idea. Rather, it is a material reality based in historical fact that is in the mix along with everything else, including what we believe or are aware of.

But first, take a moment to write and think about what you've just read.

WRITE AND REFLECT

What do you think about the idea that identity is something you can take on or off?

By contrast, what do you think about the idea that what you are has already been determined and doesn't change?

IDENTITIES

> *It would seem that Our Lord finds our desires not too strong, but too weak. We are half-hearted creatures, fooling about with drink and sex and ambition when infinite joy is offered us, like an ignorant child who wants to go on making mud pies in a slum because he cannot imagine what is meant by the offer of a holiday at the sea. We are far too easily pleased.*

C.S. LEWIS, *WEIGHT OF GLORY*

Malik

I was addicted to pleasure, money, status, power and lust. I grew so dark competing with everyone, comparing what they have to what I had. There was no rest in my life; there was a constant emptiness and shallowness that could not be filled. I was idolizing other gods and there was no contentment.

As a child, I grew up in a very safe home with great parents. I have a brother that is one year older and a sister that is four years younger. My brother and I were put on a swim team when we were very young. I was very competitive, did not like to lose and took any form of losing very hard. I became very successful in swimming, was nationally ranked and had conversations with my parents about the 1988 and 1992 Olympics. At the time, I did not realize how much of my interest in swimming was because I really liked all that attention. I was only ten years old at the time. All the attention was not dealt with appropriately, and I grew addicted to it.

As I got older, I got sick and fell out of swimming. Along with that I began middle school where I was teased a lot for my big ears, big front teeth and my sickly appearance due to terrible allergies. Rejection from my peers taught me to become very observant of others' flaws and aware of my position in the pecking order. I would analyze a person, looking for their physical flaws constantly. If I was teased I would point out nuances of their physical appearance they may have never noticed.

I was a fallen sports star (kind of), a sick, goofy teenager who was consumed with status and the material world. I would constantly compare myself to others and use sarcasm, humour, wit, gossip and conformism to gain popularity to try and achieve what I knew was possible when swimming was a part of my life.

ASPECTS OF IDENTITY

A positive identity can bring focus to your life, and you may have more than one. For example, a person may be a mum, dad, son or daughter. They may be an engineer or a student, a social worker, an executive or an entrepreneur. They may be athletic, academic or musical. They might consider themselves to be a spiritual person.

Because a sense of identity is so powerful, it is easy to see how some might think their value resides in their identity (who they are). After all, they are living that identity out each and every day at home, work or school, and in their social circles both online and in real life. It is how people know and relate to them. They get rewarded when their performance of these identities meets expectations, and that of course is what most people strive for. But when they don't perform well enough, there are often consequences.

Herein lies the problem with placing our value in our identity. It only works when the pressure isn't too great and our performance is acceptable. The moment we are overwhelmed, our identity and value can be overwhelmed with it.

There are probably many ways to think about these kinds of high-stakes identity games. But four varieties of identity I'd like us to think about are achieved identities (accomplishments), inherited identities (family/background/DNA), projected identities (social media/image) and negative identities. In some ways, these forms of identity will overlap and reinforce one another but we'll look at each to understand their allure, and the potentially destructive impact of placing your sense of value and well-being in your ability to perform them to the satisfaction of others.

ACHIEVED IDENTITIES

The wealthy businessman, John D. Rockefeller, was once asked, 'How much money is enough?' to which he is supposed to have replied, 'Just a little bit more.'

This is the motto of people who struggle with placing their worth in their achieved identity. The motivation here is different from pride or greed. It is instead a need to prove value through accomplishment. It is the hope that a certain job title, educational accomplishment or reputation will fill the emptiness inside. But, like Mr Rockefeller, they usually find that whatever they achieve, it is never enough.

For that reason, a person who struggles to achieve worth through success may become a workaholic. They can become victims of the so-called 'hedonic treadmill'. They know no lasting peace, driving themselves to achieve more and more, to attain more and more, only feeling as good as their latest achievement or compliment – the afterglow of which quickly fades – followed by cravings for another 'hit' of accomplishment and recognition.

This is a grace-less, performance-driven way to live. It devalues those who do not make achievement their main goal in life and overvalues those of higher status. People who live this way are willing to use others and break or bend rules in order to get what they think will make them whole.

While such people may indeed climb the ladder of success, their sense of value is always in jeopardy because no one is completely insulated from the possibility of an error in judgment.

Achieved identities and the temporary sense of significance or security they afford are always at risk of being damaged or lost in a broken world filled with temptations and hurt people bound to make mistakes – especially when, as their status, power and wealth increase, they become less and less accountable to others.

One only need look at recent headlines in the news to find examples of people whose error in judgment on social media, or moment of weakness with someone they were inappropriately attracted to, led to them losing everything they had worked so hard to attain. I could offer several current examples such as people in the film industry, news media, politicians, religious personalities, sports stars or corporate executives; but there is no need. In whatever time you are reading this, I predict that plenty of recent examples will readily come to mind.

Lessons from Scripture

Scripture reflects this reality, 'As dead flies give perfume a bad smell, so a little folly outweighs wisdom and honor' (Ecclesiastes 10:1 NIV). As does common sense; as Benjamin Franklin is known to have said, 'It takes many good deeds to build a good reputation, and only one bad one to lose it.'

The bottom line is that rooting your identity in things of this world is not secure. Paul warns Timothy against this, writing,

> *Command those who are rich in this world's goods not to be haughty or to set their hope on riches, which are uncertain, but on God who richly provides us with all things for our enjoyment. Tell them to do good, to be rich in good deeds, to be generous givers, sharing with others. In this way they will save up a treasure for themselves as a firm foundation for the future and so lay hold of what is truly life.*

1 TIMOTHY 6:17–19

This is, of course, an echo of Jesus's famous exhortation to build our lives on the solid rock of his word, rather than on the sinking sand of our own desires (Matthew 7:24–27).

INHERITED IDENTITIES

Some people find their value in their family background, the social class they were born into or their ethnicity, status or position. They may think they are better than others because they are physically attractive, capable or naturally athletic. If they find themselves born into a position of privilege, they may think they are better than others, making them prideful and arrogant. They may mistakenly think that they are untouchable or entitled to special treatment because of their looks, status or wealth.

Conversely, if they were born into a disadvantaged family, or a body that is deemed by others to be less capable or attractive, they may think they have no value. They may mistakenly believe there is no hope for change, or that they are worth less than others. This devalues God's handiwork in making them and cripples the purpose for which they were made.

I am not suggesting that the family or body a person is born into won't affect them in life. It will. Our start in life will either come with or without access to certain resources. But in neither case does a person's value depend upon the family or body they were born into. All of us are beautiful and capable in our own special way and have something to offer the world. Though no one else may see it, God does, and he has a plan for your life.

Lessons from Scripture

Misplaced value in family of origin was a belief Jesus challenged in the Jews. They believed that their salvation came from the fact that they were God's chosen people. This was their inherited identity. The problem was that God's choosing them had nothing to do with them being better than others. It was by his grace that he chose them, based on his loyal love – not any special quality they had. Furthermore, this way of thinking stood in the way of God's ultimate plan to bring hope and salvation to the whole world through Jesus.

That is why Jesus said to the disciples:

'If anyone comes to me and does not hate his own father and mother, and wife and children, and brothers and sisters, and even his own life, he cannot be my disciple.'

LUKE 14:26

For some this is a troublesome passage. Jesus preached that we are to love one another, ourselves, our enemies, and to honour our mother and father (Luke 6:27–38; Luke 10:27–8; Luke 18:20). These commands seem to be in conflict with the command to 'hate' one's family, but they are not. In Luke 14:26, Jesus is letting the Jews know that they could no longer rely on their identification as God's chosen people – their inherited identity – to make them righteous. They needed to utterly reject – hate – this way of thinking, because it led to pride. Instead, he wanted them to identify themselves through a personal relationship with him through grace – a relationship that would soon become available to everyone, everywhere.

Similarly, we must realize that whatever sort of family, body, privilege or disadvantage we are born into, we are all equal at the foot of the cross. All are worth enough to die for. All in need of a Saviour.

Jesus demonstrated this by spending time with those who were considered outcasts or of low social position. He elevated and ministered to women at a time when the culture restrained them from participating in roles they were created to play. He healed those who were sick and struggling with disabilities as an inspiration to others, touched and ate with those who were considered unclean or of low social position.

Conversely, he chastised those held in high esteem: the Pharisees, teachers of the law and scribes. Not because they were inherently bad, but because of their pride and arrogance. They had closed off their hearts to the God who gave them their position of trust and influence. They placed their value in their accomplishments and capabilities, rather than recognizing their need for God's grace … just like everyone else.

PROJECTED IDENTITIES

The person who bases their value in their projected identity relies upon their public image to feel good about themselves. This could include job title or social position. This person lives on compliments. They use people to evoke words of praise like a person struggling with a crack addiction uses a pipe. They will quickly conform to the ideals of the group to gain acceptance. Vulnerability frightens them. They would rather project the appearance of being OK and maintenance-free because they want to give the impression that they have it all together.

They probably compare themselves with others to see how they measure up. They want to maintain their public image at any price, because losing it means losing their identity and basis of value. They may ruminate on interactions they've had with others for hours or even days, hoping that their image hasn't been tarnished, trying to discern what others think of them.

They may exhibit false pride, meaning that while they are outwardly braggadocious, they don't truly believe what they say about themselves. They appraise others with the same critical eye they use to appraise themselves. At the same time, they are people pleasers, living or dying by compliments or attention. They feed on success or public recognition.

Lessons from Scripture

The Apostle Paul, in his letter to the Galatians (1:10) sets out to make the case that he would not have had the ministry he had if his goal was to please others. He had, in many cases, done the opposite. He laid down his status and position as a Pharisee and Hebrew of Hebrews (Philippians 3:4–7) because he saw them as a distraction to what was truly important and valuable – knowing Christ and following him in this life and into the next.

To know Jesus is to implicitly understand that our value is not in the face we present to the world. He was the King of Kings and yet he came to us in the form of a defenceless human baby, born into an impoverished home, his birth announced by shepherds of low social status. In spite of the optics through which the world may have viewed him, his Father knew who he was and inspired kings and angels to attend to him, to the wonder and amazement of those present.

As he grew, time after time, Jesus refused to do what would garner him favour with authorities, say what people wanted him to say or look like people wanted him to look. Not because he was obstinate or a troublemaker, but because he could do only what the Father told him to do, based on who he was and the purpose for which he came. This is a theme we will expand upon in the next chapter.

(SELF-)SERVANTS

This is a subset of projected identities that is worthy of mention. (Self-)Servants are people who go into a profession, or make it their job, to serve or care for others in order to gain a sense of value. The problem is not what they do, but why they do it. It is a question of motivation, which ultimately is about them. This is a chronic problem amongst doctors, nurses, psychologists, pastors, missionaries and charity workers. What better proof that you are worth something than to have other people tell you how helpful and wonderful you are?

I have struggled with this myself. Hopefully though, I've learned something about it by now, and here's what it is:

Those who have misplaced their value in being a carer are, in actuality, only giving to get what they need – a worldly reputation (that is easily lost), and a (temporary) sense of worth. In fact, if this is you then it is critical to recognize that you are not actually 'giving' at all. You are only renting a sense of security or significance that you do not own. You may find that you become exhausted as you strive to continue to make the monthly payments on your identity (and value) as 'the selfless, kind, giving, reliable one' by continuing to say 'yes' to everyone, lest you disappoint someone. You will do more and more for others, staying longer than you intended, giving more than you can afford. In the process, you may wind up taking from others in your life – usually time and attention from family or friends – in order to give to others. This will look like dedication and sacrificial giving on the outside, and that is why it is so beguiling. However, if allowed to go on unchecked it can lead to resentment, burnout, broken relationships at home and other unhealthy coping mechanisms.

The most extreme version of this dynamic is known as Munchausen by Proxy Syndrome, wherein a person will deliberately make another person sick, often by poisoning them, so that they can garner sympathy and forge identity as the selfless caregiver.

In recovery circles, these traits are known as co-dependency or emotional dependency. A cognitive behavioural therapist might say this person struggles with dysfunctional beliefs. A psychoanalyst might say that this person lacks ego strength. And a pastor might say that this person has been deceived by the enemy into thinking that their value is dependent on what others think of them.

It is critical to correct this. Because on top of misplaced value and the problems that go with it, it can affect our judgment with the people we serve. They come to us for help with their problems and to find new, creative ways to reach *their* goals. Our relationship is meant to be about helping them. Not to get them to help us with our value issues.

It's not that helping others doesn't feel good. It does – it feels great and is a worthy calling! But doing it in order to elicit praise from others so that we can feel valuable can't be our primary motivation. If it is, then it's really about us, not them, or him.

Lessons from Scripture

The tricky thing about the '(Self-)Servant' identity is that, in balance and moderation, some of these qualities might be admirable or useful. The Bible is full of sacrificial people who followed God wholeheartedly, Jesus himself being the ultimate example. Dedication, sometimes to the extreme, is often necessary to achieve difficult goals. There may also be seasons where other relationships need to be put on hold or limited in order to make room for something that demands a bit more effort for a time. And, Scripture says,

> *A good name is more desirable than great riches;*
> *to be esteemed is better than silver or gold.*

PROVERBS 22:1 NIV

But, of course, the trademark recipe of the enemy is to take a little bit of truth, sprinkle in some lies, stir it all together, bake and then serve up the poison. Tastes good going down but, in the end, it leads to death.

The key question to ask yourself is: what is my motivation for this behaviour and attitude? Jesus gave out of an overflow of the security and significance he found in the Father. He knew what he was – that is, the Son of God filled with intrinsic worth and value in relationship to the Father. Who he was and what he did flowed naturally from that.

He fills us up. We pour it out. That's how it's meant to work.

NEGATIVE IDENTITIES

It may have occurred to you that these first three types of identity are generally considered to be socially acceptable. As long as people are fitting in and meeting expectations they will be praised, rewarded and encouraged. And as long as the encouragement keeps coming, people will often be able to cope with the pressure that comes with performing and maintaining their image and status.

But some go the other way. They turn to escape strategies to cope with the pressures of life. This might include sex, pornography, drugs, alcohol, shopping or gambling. They will then begin to identify themselves with these activities. They join subcultures that come with ways of dressing and acting. Many of these subcultures also have their own vocabulary, customs and values that help identify those who 'know' from those who don't. Membership in these groups means acceptance, which heightens their allure. You want to be with your friends, doing what they do and feeling what they feel. You feel that outsiders don't understand, and that you share a kind of secret knowledge.

While these cotton candy temptations offer a temporary reprieve, they only highlight the emptiness once the distraction has ended. And sometimes these feel-good distractions leave a trail of destruction in their wake, making the reality you come back to worse than when you left it. Lost jobs, broken relationships, alienation from others, health problems, financial problems, legal problems, unresolved grief and a future that looks increasingly bleak are the usual outcomes to this approach.

Membership in such groups ultimately must come to an end. People grow too old for them, overdose, are arrested or encounter relationship problems. The band breaks up, leaving us older and alone with nothing but memories of the years behind us and perhaps some significant regrets.

Self-harming behaviours are not uncommon amongst people

with negative self-worth. Physical pain offers a distraction from their deeper emotional pain. A fast, accessible way to feel something different. To refocus the pain. Even suicidal behaviour can be thought of as a maladaptive problem-solving strategy. Often though, this tragic choice comes less from a desire to truly die, than it does from an effort to escape everything that is broken and wrong.

Lessons from Scripture

James writes,

> *But each one is tempted when he is lured and enticed by his own desires. Then when desire conceives, it gives birth to sin, and when sin is full grown, it gives birth to death.*

JAMES 1:14–15

While the other identities can ultimately be just as destructive in less obvious ways, negative identities are marked by the obvious and often dramatic toll they take upon those who hold them. Anyone who has ministered to others in counselling, pastoral or recovery settings understands the devastation those who struggle with low self-worth can inflict upon themselves through the behavioural or chemical addictions they've chosen in an attempt to self-medicate. Consistent with James' admonition, in their stories are many kinds of death. Death of relationships, potential futures, hopes, dreams – even their brain and body's natural pleasure system, which is meant to reinforce healthy social and physical interaction, may have 'died' and needs to be resurrected again in order to begin to function properly. This condition, known as 'anhedonia', means the person struggling with addiction is unable to experience pleasure in ways that are not chemically induced. They have to rewire their brain to experience pleasure again in healthy ways through continual engagement with healthy activities and ways of thinking, regardless of how they feel about it. This process is daunting and can take a long time – some don't make it. And unfortunately, there have been too many times when people struggling with a negative identity have made choices to cope with the pain that have led to actual physical death.

If we want to grow, then we must let go of the idea that our value is in our performance, image, problems or in what others think about us.

Not only is it not true, but it is not a peaceful way to live, nor is there any eternal reward in it. Even if a person manages to walk the tightrope of public perfection their whole lives, time will eventually take its toll as they pass on all their roles and authority to someone else after they have left this world for the next. And death is just one of those facts of life. (Sorry to be a downer. I don't like it either. But I didn't make it up. We are all confronted with it and there's no escape.)

Solomon puts it this way:

> *For a person may labor with wisdom, knowledge and skill, and then they must leave all they own to another who has not toiled for it. This too is meaningless and a great misfortune.*

ECCLESIASTES 2:21 NIV

Ultimately, all worldly identities will be lost. None of them last. We simply cannot take the contents of our bank account, our degrees, possessions, title or reputations with us when we pass from this world.

However, if worth, meaning, acceptance and peace is what we want, then our misguided strategies to find value must die for us to truly live. In other words, if we don't kill them, it is only a matter of time before they kill us .... Or, at least, leave us with a significant limp. They won't die easy, I know. It may be very, very painful. I hope and pray you survive it – and you can survive it – though the current structure of your life may well not survive.

That is why we often don't enter recovery or counselling. We don't become brutally honest with ourselves until we absolutely have to. Until the police are at the door. The wife is leaving. The boss is threatening to fire you. The doctor is calling. Or your friends finally get fed up and stop calling or accepting your calls.

But there is a God who values you for who you truly are, flaws and all. And likely, there are people made in his image that will do the same. In fact, your flaws may become your most attractive, redeeming quality, because they will fuel your grace towards others as you become humbly dependent on God's grace towards you.

WRITE AND REFLECT

When are you tempted to place your value in your achievements, or the opinions of others about you?

Where does the pressure to 'escape' come from in your life?

How does that affect you?

What coping strategies do you use?

CHAPTER 3

WHAT YOU ARE: THE FOUNDATION

They will be like a tree planted by the water
that sends out its roots by the stream.
It does not fear when heat comes;
its leaves are always green.
It has no worries in a year of
drought and never fails to bear fruit.

JEREMIAH 17:8 NIV

HOW WE WERE MADE

It is worth taking time to review what God's word says about the way in which we were made, and how we got from there to here.

To begin with, according to Scripture, all human beings – regardless of their belief system – are made in God's image; a mixture of earth and Spirit (Genesis 1:26–27, Genesis 5:1–2). That is *what* we are. We didn't do anything to earn this and couldn't possibly do anything to disqualify ourselves from it or run away from it.

It is a gift from God that he made human beings in his likeness. People often forget that in the beginning, long before the Fall, we were called 'good' by God and he blessed us (Genesis 1:28, 31). Then God made Eve to be in relationship with himself and with Adam, and Scripture says that they were naked and unashamed (Genesis 2:25). There was no serpent yet. No one had taken a bite of the apple. Everything was as it was meant to be.

This is very important.

We were made to be blessed, free, with no secrets, no shame and in a love relationship with God and with one another. It also describes the bedrock of human worth: we are inherently valuable because we are image bearers, male and female, of the God who made us.

That is one aspect of what a human being is. Here's another: flashing forward in the story of humanity, Scripture also tells us that Jesus died not just for the righteous, but also for the ungodly (Romans 5:6–8), so that all might have a chance to be reconciled to him. In other words, Jesus thought that all of us, whether we followed him or not, or would ever follow him or not, were worth dying for.

Note that this is true regardless of what we believe about God, what we have done, or what has been done to us. This value has been built into us from the start. It is the second part of what we are. We are valuable, and we do not depreciate. Our value, our loveability, is innate, whatever situation you may find yourself in. You are worth enough to die for. No matter how you have struggled. Whatever else you may have done or are doing. Whatever has been done to you.

It is significant that, well after the Fall, Scripture still affirms that man is (still) made in the image of God (1 Corinthians 11:7, James 3:9). Yes, everyone since Adam and Eve was born into an entanglement with sin, but your value is still in there, capable of being progressively disentangled from sin through a relationship with Jesus and the ongoing, intra-active work of the Holy Spirit. There will be highs and lows, twists and turns, on this journey. Don't expect it to be linear. It's not.

It was after God – a real being who actually created people in his image at a point in time – blessed Adam and Eve and called them 'good', that the enemy slithered in and corrupted the creation with lies, motivated by a bruised pride. And it was then that Adam and Eve began hiding, filled with the knowledge that they, for the first time, had done something that was wrong (Genesis 3:7). Instead of naked and unashamed, they were filled with shame, and so they covered themselves and hid.

Dr Marsha Linehan, who developed Dialectical Behavioural Therapy,[8] writes that the emotion of shame signals to someone that they have done something so bad, so contrary to the rules of the group they belong to, that they themselves are bad and will therefore be rejected. If that's true, then Genesis gives us the first account of someone who felt a false sense of shame, because while Adam and Eve did have to leave the Garden, they certainly were not rejected by God. If they were, God would have abandoned them and left them hiding behind their insufficient covering. Instead, what did God do? He went looking for them!

He had not cut off relationship with them. He had not stopped loving them. They were not worth any less. There were harsh consequences for their behaviour because their new knowledge of both good and evil set off an intra-active web of events that sedimented itself into them and us. However, even after their choices led to them being expelled from the garden so that they might not do even more damage, God made them more suitable clothing (Genesis 3:21), blessed them with three children for which they were grateful (Genesis 4:1, 25), and allowed Adam to live a long life (Genesis 5:3).

Importantly, even in the curse, he makes the promise of salvation through the 'offspring' of the woman who will one day crush the head of the enemy and rectify the damage of sin to the world and its people (Genesis 3:15). It is also telling about the nature of their continued relationship that Adam and Eve still seemed to love God and acknowledge him as their Lord after they left the garden.

In short, God's connection with Adam and Eve remained, and they relished this connection. He didn't stop loving them, value them less or abandon them, nor they him, even as they experienced the consequences of their behaviour.

---

8 Marsha Linehan, *Cognitive-Behavioral Treatment of Borderline Personality Disorder* (Guilford Press, 1993).

WHAT YOU HAVE: HIS ATTRIBUTES

Bonnie

My whole life had been with alcohol. I thought my marriage was based on it. I thought that without alcohol we would never connect. I thought I wouldn't be funny, and my life would be so boring. I was terrified and anxious; even in church and Bible study the fear would come that I would never please God if I kept choosing alcohol over him.

God spoke to me and said he loved me whether drunk or sober, but I had asked for more of him and the journey we were about to hike needed a lighter backpack. I needed to take alcohol off my back and he would take me places I never imagined, like here and now. On 2 July 2010, I quit drinking. I believe God healed me. I depended on him through each quiet time every morning, and still meet with him daily. We are tight.

We are a masterpiece splattered with red paint by an intrusive madman. A beautiful sunset obscured by thunderclouds. An innocent child infected with a curable disease. A boxer's glorious, shattered smile. Brennan Manning, a writer and follower of Christ who struggled with alcohol, says it well, 'Aristotle said I am a rational animal; I say I am an angel with an incredible capacity for beer.'[9]

Because of the explosive combination of factors in her background, Bonnie made the mistake of thinking that what she was, was based on her relationship with alcohol. What she came to realize was that, all this time, she had only ever been what God created her to be. Worth enough to die for and made in his image.

Mixed in with all of our struggles and all of the damage are the attributes of God. We long for justice, peace, mercy, acceptance

---

9 Brennan Manning, *The Ragamuffin Gospel: Embracing the Unconditional Love of God* (Multnomah, 1990), p.25.

and purpose. We are creative. When relationships are broken, we hope for restoration and reconciliation. We desire to be a part of something bigger than ourselves. When we do something wrong, we intuitively know it.

Yes, different cultures hold different values; and yet, there are a great number of values that appear to be universally held.[10] How can this be in a world full of such beautiful diversity? I suggest it is because the same God made us all in his image, all of us reflecting him in our own way, stained or distorted though it may be as a consequence of other's choices, our choices and the sometimes-hostile environments in which we live.

This is one more aspect of our foundational value as human beings that we can never lose or have taken away. Nothing can erase or change it. He is in us for good – whether we like it or not, admit to it or not.

Because of that, you can risk being vulnerable. Share something real about yourself. Get honest about things. Whatever happens, our inherent value cannot be diminished. And we just might find that living this way, allowing ourselves to be known and connected with, even in the dark places, has its rewards.

---

10 S.H. Schwartz, *Universals in the Content and Structure of Values: Theoretical Advances and Empirical Tests in 20 Countries* (San Diego Academic Press, 1992).

WRITE AND REFLECT

What do you think of the idea that though there may be consequences for behaviour, it doesn't make us worth any less?

What aspect of God's character do you think shines most clearly in you? For example, do you love justice, care for people, etc.?

CHILDREN OF GOD

Alexa

My name is Alexa. I am a child of God that struggles with co-dependency, fear and anxiety. I found that I was so dependent on my son's behaviour and choices for my own peace and joy, that when he began to make choices contrary to those I thought he should make, I became overwhelmed with fear and anxiety to the point where I would suffer from panic attacks and depression. I would not have called myself a co-dependent until I learned what that meant in the recovery ministry about a year and a half ago.

Not everyone makes the decision to follow Christ. Being a child of God is an identity that is taken on only when one chooses to follow him. This identity is different from the others we looked at because it is a spiritual identity, not a worldly one. It is also perfectly aligned with our foundational worth and purpose and reserved solely for those who make the choice to believe in him.

Yet to all who did receive him, to those who believed in his name, he gave the right to become children of God – children born not of natural descent, nor of human decision or a husband's will, but born of God.

JOHN 1:12–13 NIV

Once you have truly made this choice, even if you were to later choose to walk away from God, he will never leave you:

For I am convinced that neither death nor life, neither angels nor demons, neither the present nor the future, nor any powers, neither height nor depth, nor anything else in all creation, will be able to separate us from the love of God that is in Christ Jesus our Lord.

ROMANS 8:38–39 NIV

Now this is the will of the one who sent me – that I should not lose one person of every one he has given me, but raise them all up at the last day.

JOHN 6:39

Once you make this choice you become intra-connected with Christ in a new way. You receive his Spirit within you. He promises to build you up through his church, the body of Christ (Ephesians 4:11–13), and to use you for a purpose (Jeremiah 29:11). Nothing in this world can erase this spiritual identity, and that is because it was not achieved by merit but given by grace (Ephesians 2:8–9).

Regardless of what has been done to you, or what mistakes you made or continue to make, God sees you. He will walk with you, empower you, love you and never leave you (Psalm 23). He is not unaffected by what happens to you and wants justice for you (Isaiah 30:18, John 11:33). We can be comforted by the love of Christ no matter who rejected us or what they said about us (John 1:12, 1 John 3:1).

He is somehow, some way, working things out for the good in ways we may never understand this side of eternity (Romans 8:28). And though he is not the author of your pain, he will seek to use it for something good, to not waste it (John 10:10).

God doesn't abandon those who love him even when we bring trouble upon ourselves. Throughout the Old Testament period when the Israelites experienced the consequences of their disobedience, God maintained an attitude of love and yearning for relationship with them. Jesus himself affirms this.

Jerusalem, Jerusalem, you who kill the prophets and stone those sent to you, how often I have longed to gather your children together, as a hen gathers her chicks under her wings, and you were not willing. Look, your house is left to you desolate ...

LUKE 13:34–35 NIV

Here we have one of the few times that we see Jesus likening his feelings for Israel to that of a mother (rather than a father), and it is a stirring image. A mother's love for her children is fierce and self-sacrificing. And yet, he also would not violate their free will by making them turn back to him when they wanted to go their own way, bringing some painful short-term consequences upon themselves.

Our identity as children of God comes with all these promises and truths that we can stack on top of our inherent worth as human beings who were made in God's image and worth enough to die for. From this rock-solid foundation, we can more readily make meaning out of our unique experiences, weaknesses, mistakes and failures.

In fact, both Christians and non-Christians can and do choose to create identities for themselves that make even painful experiences meaningful. There is a large body of literature on 'post-traumatic growth' which indicates that all people seem to have a need to do this in the wake of traumatic experience.[11] But if this 're-storying' is built on an identity that is not rooted in our inherent human worth, then it is still vulnerable to attack by the worldly forces of time, temptation, errors in judgment, ever-shifting opinions and cultural climates. Clinging to such constructions for worth or meaning is ultimately as foolish as clinging to a life jacket with a slow leak.

What we need is a foundation to build our lives on that is both in, and yet beyond, this world, and therefore invulnerable to it. Based on what and who God says we are, we can learn to forgive those who have hurt us, make amends with those we have hurt, reconcile broken relationships and establish healthy limits and boundaries when needed. Because we are inherently, innately, worth it. And because others, when they are told 'no' or asked to live within limits, are still valuable and God still has a plan and purpose for them, too. We can *all* stand on God's promise to level the mountains in our life (Isaiah 45:2) regardless of what anyone else does or thinks, and whatever worldly things we lose or gain.[12]

---

11 Richard G. Tedeschi, Lawrence G. Calhoun, 'Postraumatic Growth: Conceptual Foundation and Empirical Evidence', *Psychological Inquiry* 15, vol 1, (2004), pp. 1-18.
12 If you don't know Jesus but would like to further explore reasons to begin a relationship with him, please see Appendix 1 in the back of this book.

I know that everything God does will endure for ever; nothing can be added to it and nothing taken from it.

ECCLESIASTES 3:14 NIV

Do not store up for yourselves treasures on earth, where moths and vermin destroy, and where thieves break in and steal. But store up for yourselves treasures in heaven, where moths and vermin do not destroy, and where thieves do not break in and steal. For where your treasure is, there your heart will be also.

MATTHEW 6:19–21 NIV

EVEN IN SUFFERING

I believe like a child that suffering will be healed and made up for, that all the humiliating absurdity of human contradictions will vanish like a pitiful mirage, like the despicable fabrication of the impotent and infinitely small Euclidean mind of man, that in the world's finale, at the moment of eternal harmony, something so precious will come to pass that it will suffice for all hearts, for the comforting of all resentments, for the atonement of all the crimes of humanity, for all the blood that they've shed; that it will make it not only possible to forgive but to justify all that has happened.

FYODOR DOSTOEVSKY, *THE BROTHERS KARAMAZOV*

Theo

It was during primary school that you could say I first put my faith in Jesus Christ for my salvation. Yet outside of my relationship with my grandmother, I do not have any strong feelings of connection or being loved unconditionally while growing up.

In school I struggled to find my identity and became defined by what I did instead of who God had created me to be. I developed an overbite and buck teeth that would take five years of braces and headgear to correct, and I was soon left behind in both physical development and athletic ability. Which is a nice way to say I was small and uncoordinated. I tried to play baseball, basketball and football, hoping to find my niche but struggling in each. One baseball game stands out, which my girlfriend attended. We were losing by a few runs when I got up to bat during the last inning. There were two outs and no one on base. Not being all that great a batter to begin with, combined with the stress of the final out while my girlfriend was watching in the stands, I struck out to end the game.

As I walked back to the dugout with my head down, my team mates hurled insults and clearly communicated that I was the reason we had lost the game. After handshakes with the winning team, I looked around for my girlfriend, but she was gone. Someone said she went to the neighbourhood pool, so I got on my bike and rode to the pool across the car park. We were not members, so I tried to talk to her through the fence. She sent her friends over to tell me we were no longer 'going steady'. I begged her friends to convince her to come talk to me, but their response was 'You'll probably just strike out again.'

Regardless of what we believe about God, there will be times when we experience a sense of meaninglessness, loneliness, doubt, anxiety, anger or fear. We may have relationship problems, or be haunted by regret, shame or pain from the past. Others will attack us or try to hurt us – sometimes it will be because of our faith and the things we stand for.

This should not surprise us because Jesus told us it would happen.

If the world hates you, be aware that it hated me first. If you belonged to the world, the world would love you as its own. However, because you do not belong to the world, but I chose you out of the world, for this reason the world hates you ... But I have told you these things so that when their time comes, you will remember that I told you about them ...

JOHN 15:18-19, 16:4

But those who have put their faith in Christ can rely on the truth that these circumstances won't define you or diminish your spiritual identity or eternal destiny. That is the thing to remember right after that fight with your friend, family member, spouse or partner. In the midst of the fear of losing your job. Hearing you've failed your course. Added yet another debt collection letter to the stack. Received hard news about your health. Just after you have been rejected ... again.

It's easy to feel confident in your identity when life is good and the sun is shining. It is much more difficult when you're going through your own Job experience (Job 1:13–2:12) – when all has been lost, stolen, infected or senselessly destroyed.

The ultimate example of what it looks like to not allow yourself to be defined by your circumstances, or by what others say about you or do to you, is found in Jesus' experience, standing before Pontius Pilate during his trial:

... 'Where do you come from?' he asked Jesus, but Jesus gave him no answer. 'Do you refuse to speak to me?' Pilate said. 'Don't you realize I have power either to free you or to crucify you?' Jesus answered, 'You would have no power over me if it were not given to you from above ...'

JOHN 19:9-11 NIV

Consider the context: Jesus had been betrayed by Peter, whipped, beaten, abandoned – the people who welcomed him into Jerusalem as though he were a conquering king earlier that week were now outside Pilate's court chanting for him to be crucified. Given a choice between setting him free, or Barabbas who had murdered someone, they preferred Barabbas. Jesus was utterly alone and rejected by everyone.

Yet despite all that, as he stands there before Pilate, surrounded by symbols of Roman power, he tells Pilate that he has no power except what has been given to him from above. This is an astonishing statement! It certainly appears to be false on the surface of things. Yet Jesus is clearly not focused on Pilate's power, or on escaping his circumstances to find freedom, or on what the chanting crowd outside is saying about him, or on how all his friends had abandoned him – even Peter, who had so boldly pledged allegiance earlier that very morning.

Instead, he is focused on the power of his Father, his identity in his Father and his purpose in life. He knows what and who he is, why he was sent and what he has to do. He is suffering, yet steadfast; his path flowing from what and who he knows himself to be.

That is why he can muster the courage to say to his accuser in the midst of torture, 'You would have no power over me if it were not given to you from above.'

Importantly, Jews in Jesus' time looked at his suffering as a repudiation of his claim to be the Messiah. They thought that if he was who he said he was, then he wouldn't be facing such resistance. This is because, in Old Testament times, God's people were under the Deuteronomic system of blessings for obedience and curses for disobedience.

Understandably then, up until the time of Jesus, Jews saw a prosperous person and thought that they must be living an upright life. If catastrophe struck, they reasoned that this must have been brought on by some unrepented, hidden sin.

Job's friends jumped to this conclusion. Yet even under the old covenant, Job came to understand that his tragedy was not due to his own personal sin. He concluded that, ultimately, God's reasons for allowing what he allowed were unfathomable from his finite perspective, from which he could not appreciate the eternal realities of the spiritual realms (Job 42:3). To explain why his terrible suffering was allowed by an all-good, all-powerful God would be like trying to explain trigonometry to a goldfish.

So, of course, when Jesus was arrested and tortured, the Jews thought that he couldn't be the Messiah. He was not experiencing blessing, so must have been a liar. A sinner so blasphemous they actually tore their robes over it.

What they failed to recognize is that Jesus was ushering in a Covenant of Grace with a God who has always been gracious with his people. Like Jesus, we too have been sent by the Father, created with inherent worth, made in his image, rooted in our identification with him and built for a purpose. Even if we lose status, power, friendships or family – as Jesus did – our value and identity in the Lord is still secure. There is still a purpose in our lives.

It may even be that the adversity we face is in some unfathomable way a part of our equipping, our badge of qualification, for the work we will be called to do. The thing that allows us to look another hurting person in the eye and say, 'I get it', and because there's just something about the way you say it, they believe you.

Deanna

The night I planned to carry out my death wish, I lay flat on the floor, exhausted from crying but relieved the pain would be over soon. This is when I distinctly encountered Christ in a very personal way. I saw his face in my mind and heard him firmly and gently say, 'That is not my plan for you.' He said this twice and then faded away. I simply gave up my suicide plan and went to bed.

The next day, I decided this was too much for me to handle alone and finally sought medical help, even though it went against my legalistic reading of Scripture that anti-depressants were for people with little faith. Christ had made it clear I was not to die, so I finally became willing to compromise and seek help. I'm so glad I did!

I took anti-depressants for six years and I believe they saved my life while God continued to work on my belief systems. It is incredible to me to think that now, after several years of working through these issues, I have come to a place where I am able to sponsor and lead women who are going through the same kinds of things I did. I am growing as I observe God work powerfully in the lives of others through me!

I am deeply mindful that some who are reading this may be experiencing terrible suffering or conflict or know someone who is. So let me say again that I am not in any way minimizing your pain or glorifying your circumstances.

It is just that, inevitably in life, suffering will come. It can be traumatizing – and one essential element of the traumatic is that when you are in it, you have no words to describe it. By the time you are able to begin to describe it, you are beginning to move out of it and get some distance from it. When it is happening, it just envelops and resists identification. Even Jesus in the garden, or on the cross feeling forsaken by the Father, seemed to have moments when he was adrift in fear and pain due to the limitations he placed upon his own omniscience (Mark 15:34).

When pain and suffering do come, clinging to what and who we are, our eternal purpose can provide the strength to persevere. Regardless of what our partner, spouse, children, parents, siblings, boss, teacher, neighbour, co-worker or friends think about us. Regardless of whether we are facing sickness or health, a break-up or reconciliation, financial gain or loss, employment or unemployment, success or failure, life or death. To know that whatever is not healed in this life will be healed and put right in the next, and even the hope that somehow, some way, from an eternal perspective where we can see how God used it, it will eventually make sense and it will be worth the pain and struggle.

If you can't hear that right now, that is completely OK. I just spoke to someone who went through a very painful family tragedy about ten years ago, and they are only just now beginning to see something redeeming in it. Still, I'm sure they would rather it never happened in the first place. We would all rather be healthy and together, if it were possible. Sometimes, though, it just isn't possible – at least not in this life.

It's doubtful that any of us will be able to achieve trust in the process to the extent that Jesus did – especially during periods of acute pain and suffering. But we can pursue it. Paul did, and seems to have achieved some measure of it, as he described in his letter to the Philippians,

> ... I have learned to be content whatever the circumstances. I know what it is to be in need, and I know what it is to have plenty. I have learned the secret of being content in any and every situation, whether well fed or hungry, whether living in plenty or in want. I can do all this through him who gives me strength.

PHILIPPIANS 4:11–13 NIV

Perhaps the best we can do is trust him to see us through the dark times, even when we don't see a way forward. To look to his word, his presence, his people and his good gifts to bring us comfort. To believe, by faith, that he won't waste our pain or loss and that someday, he will redeem it.

WRITE AND REFLECT

Can you think of a time when you experienced suffering, and all seemed lost? What happened?

Have you made any sense or meaning of that time of suffering?

What has it forced you to appreciate, or motivated you to do that you otherwise wouldn't have?

How would it have struck you if, during your time of suffering, someone had suggested that somehow God would use it for good?

It's one thing to talk about struggles in our past we have since overcome, and another to talk about ongoing struggles that are not yet resolved. How do you feel about sharing your present struggles with someone else when you aren't yet sure how it will turn out?

CHAPTER 4

STRENGTH FROM WEAKNESS

There is nothing on earth that does not show either the wretchedness of man, or the mercy of God; either the weakness of man without God, or the strength of man with God.

BLAISE PASCAL, *PASCAL'S PENSÉES*

It is one thing to experience compassion intellectually, or even to give it. It is quite another thing to receive compassion when one knows that all one is entitled to is justice.

THE ASCENT OF A LEADER[13]

Laura

Early on in marriage, I struggled to find myself. In a short period of time, I had become someone's wife, someone's mother, in a strange city with no friends. I began striving to serve God with all my heart and felt that I could carve out my own place where I mattered. I worked hard at creating the good, Christian life. The image that comes to mind is that of a painter. I was masterfully painting the portrait of my life. When a dark smudge would appear on the canvas of my

---

13 Bill Thrall, Bruce McNicol, Ken McElrath, *The Ascent of a Leader: How Ordinary Relationships Develop Extraordinary Character and Influence* (Jossey-Bass, 1999), p.56.

life, I would just paint over it. I did this through striving and serving God. Someone recently said that in our unhealthiness, we either use positive flesh or negative flesh. This was positive flesh ... yet still the flesh. The rewards were immediate and much better than the black smudges ... I felt better about my canvas and myself. I see now two basic and dangerous problems that at the time I was oblivious to: fear and control. I was afraid of not having a life that others would aspire to, so I worked hard to create one. I was afraid that people wouldn't really love the real me, so I created a much lovelier version. I just kept painting. Really, I was unaware that so often I was trading true intimacy with Christ for people's approval of me.

In your weaknesses lie your greatest potential for strength and lasting life change. This is a really important concept to grasp, and it is completely other-worldly and counter-intuitive, so it merits a bit more attention.

Laura eventually came to discover that her value with God was safe no matter what anyone thought of her, and from that foundation of security she could get honest with others about what was really going on in her life. With that knowledge, she could finally put the paintbrush down, and rest.

One spiritual truth I've tried to make clear in previous chapters is that we can risk being honest with ourselves, God and others. Why? Because we are secure and significant even though we have struggles and challenges. We will, at times, face adversity, and if we can't connect with others in that space of struggle, then we will struggle alone. And alone is not a good place to be in a fight.

It could be some area of our lives that just isn't going how we would like it to, and we know God is asking us to address it. It could be an issue that isn't debilitating but has left us compensating in some way that is unhelpful or ineffective. Something from our past that we want to resolve. A painful relational issue. An unhelpful or unwanted character trait. A challenging situation in our workplace. Something someone we care about is going through that affects us deeply. An unrealized goal or desire.

Perhaps we are nowhere near rock bottom and are, in fact, quite functional – even though there may be one or two things we'd like to tweak. Or, perhaps we have hit rock bottom and know, for certain, that we need to make a change. Or, perhaps we're somewhere in between, free falling and hearing the thuds of others hitting bottom in the distance – a fate we'd like to avoid if possible.

Whatever the case, God wants to do something in our hearts and lives, and through us he wants to make an impact upon the lives of others. But the change begins in us, and it can begin only when we acknowledge whatever it is in our lives that isn't getting us where we want to go.

If we have tried and failed in the past, it doesn't mean change isn't possible. In fact, trying and failing may have actually been necessary in order to increase our motivation and open us up to new ideas and resources. As the saying goes, if our way of doing things was going to be successful, then it would have been by now. But it didn't. So it won't. No matter how many times we try it, or how much we want it to work. Trying the same broken strategies over and over is pointless. It's time to look elsewhere for the power to change.

In fact, when we find ourselves in this position, the only honest and logical thing to do is to face the facts and admit that our way of doing and thinking isn't working. And what that means, functionally speaking, is that we are powerless over whatever it is that we have been trying unsuccessfully to change. Perhaps this seems self-defeating; and in a way, it is. Because your 'self' needs to be defeated. It is your 'self' – your way of thinking and doing things, the way that seemed right to you – that got you into this position in the first place.

DEALING WITH IT

Scripture says, 'There is a way that seems right to a person, but its end is the way that leads to death' (Proverbs 14:12), and, 'In those days Israel had no king. Each man did what he considered to be right.' (Judges 21:25).

If you're not familiar with the book of Judges, it documents a time in Israel's history when God's people abandoned his way of doing things for their own. They adopted pagan idols, participated in deplorable worship practices, suffered one military and moral defeat after the next and were enslaved and oppressed as a result. Each time they found themselves in trouble and repented, God rescued them, only for them to fall back into old habits and need to be rescued again. Despite the cycle they were stuck in, God's loyal love for them never ran out.

He loves you in the exact same way. No matter how many mistakes you make, no matter how many times you've made a plan to change and failed, you have value in the eyes of God. You are significant and made of good stuff. Nothing can or ever will change that. However, it is time to turn away from the things we've become entangled with and turn our lives and will in this issue completely over to God. That means first confessing to God what is going on, and then becoming at least willing to do the things he calls us to, in order to deal with the situation (more on the details of that in the pages ahead). This is what it means to repent.

That word, 'repent', is not so popular in our culture today. However, it only means 'to turn away from' whatever it is that you are repenting of.

> *Actually, repentance is the price required for learning in any domain – it's just that outside the church it's called unlearning, whereas inside the church it's called repentance.*

ALAN HIRSCH[14]

---

14 Alan Hirsch, 5Q: *Activating the Original Intelligence and Capacity of the Body of Christ* (100 Movements, 2017), p.xxiii.

If we don't repent and surrender our life and will in this issue to God, we will remain a closed system. Working on our own power. Unwilling to let in outside resources that conflict with our way of doing things. Things that seem backward, difficult, illogical or just distasteful to us.

A secular version of this concept is found within dialectical behavioural therapy, which draws from Eastern philosophy. It's called radical acceptance, and it involves surrendering our will and desires to the impersonal universe, abandoning ourselves to whatever might come. While this idea may bring peace in the present moment for some, if there is no God, and no heaven, then our short lives are ultimately meaningless, since any meaning we create for them, and anything we will ever do, will one day devolve into meaninglessness, worm food and eventually, space dust (see the entire book of Ecclesiastes).

On the other hand, Jesus calls us to surrender our will and desire to him – a *personal* God, who loves you, has a plan for your life and values you, and who somehow, some way is actively working to redeem your situation, whether in this life or the next.

Birdie

I've come to understand that I cannot fully protect myself. Only God can do that. This is step one: powerlessness. I've never had more freedom in my life than when I fully embraced my own powerlessness. I am powerless, but God is powerful, and so there's power in powerlessness. So much of the Bible describes the power of God. Why then do I cling to some shadow of my perceived control of the way other people treat me or how things turn out? I need to stand on God's power and trust in it, and in doing so, wrap myself in the freedom of his total protection. And if he needs to defend me, he will. As Romans 8:31 says, if God is for me, who can be against me?

TRANSFORMATION

Once we admit that we are powerless, and surrender, we become open to information, energy and support that we might not have been willing to seek out or receive in the past – options we were previously unwilling to consider. "'For my thoughts are not your thoughts, neither are your ways my ways,' declares the LORD' (Isaiah 55:8 NIV).

It is paradoxical, but as the Apostle Paul said, when I admit I am weak, I am strong (2 Corinthians 12:9–10). Your admission of weakness opens your eyes to the existence of a greater strength that has a plan and power to extricate you, and those you love, from whatever you are entangled with.

> *Therefore, since we are surrounded by such a great cloud of witnesses, let us throw off everything that hinders and the sin that so easily entangles. And let us run with perseverance the race marked out for us ...*

HEBREWS 12:1 NIV

By faith, we can choose to believe that God has marked out a race for us – a good plan for our lives. Acknowledging and confronting these issues ourselves, with God, and with someone else, is a scary prospect. It will mean lowering the stoic, self-assured 'I'm fine' mask. It's risky. But the alternative is to stay stuck.

For some, it's not so much the risk of vulnerability that stops them, but the thought of losing the short-term payoff to their current thoughts, attitudes and behaviours. Something that feels good that we don't want to give up. If that sounds familiar to you, then ask God if he would help you to even *want* to change. To let go of the short-term rewards for long-term integrity and well-being.

Don't worry about your struggles disqualifying you from being used by God for amazing things. There are many, many examples of people he marked for great purpose, even though at times they violated both his commandments and human law in ways that had life-or-death consequences. Sometimes they resulted in a loss of status or position before they found their value and aligned with their transcendent purpose. These examples have been cited before by others, but are worth reviewing here:

Abraham disobeyed God by lying about Sarai being his wife and also impregnated his maidservant Hagar with Ishmael, instead of waiting for God's promised child with Sarai. Some people believe that this single act of disobedience is intra-connected with much of the unrest between Israel and other countries in the Middle East that continues to this day.

Moses murdered an Egyptian then ran off and hid in the desert for forty years.

David, a man 'after God's own heart' (Acts 13:22), committed adultery with Bathsheba, impregnated her and then had her husband killed to cover it up. Their son died, but then he and Bathsheba stayed together and out of their union came another son – the future king of Israel, Solomon.

Solomon, despite his great wisdom (1 Kings 4:29), kept a harem of non-Israelite women (a major act of disobedience), which led to the erosion of his faith. And yet, God used him to build his temple and to pen Proverbs, Ecclesiastes, Song of Songs and perhaps some of the Psalms.

Rahab made her livelihood through prostitution (and she was a Gentile during Old Testament times), yet she played a major role in Israel taking possession of the Promised Land and is listed in the book of Matthew as being in the bloodline of Jesus.

Tamar was married to Judah's son, who died, and so she cleverly posed as a prostitute to get Judah to impregnate her. For his part, Judah thought he was sleeping with a prostitute (still not much of an excuse). Both of them are also in Jesus' bloodline.

Noah apparently had a problem with alcohol, and though he knew God, he was just as much a sinner as anyone else in his time. Yet he found grace (unmerited favour) with God and was used to repopulate the earth after the flood.

Paul was an accomplice to Stephen's murder. He must have been wracked with regret and shame after the Lord miraculously revealed himself to him on the road to Damascus, but he tells us:

Brothers and sisters, I do not consider myself to have attained this. Instead I am single-minded: Forgetting the things that are behind and reaching out for the things that are ahead, ...

PHILIPPIANS 3:13

Paul found a way to put the past behind him so that God could use him for something eternal in the present. Later he writes,

I thank Christ Jesus our Lord, who has given me strength, that he considered me trustworthy, appointing me to his service. Even though I was once a blasphemer and a persecutor and a violent man, I was shown mercy because I acted in ignorance and unbelief. The grace of our Lord was poured out on me abundantly, along with the faith and love that are in Christ Jesus.

Here is a trustworthy saying that deserves full acceptance: Christ Jesus came into the world to save sinners – of whom I am the worst. But for that very reason I was shown mercy so that in me, the worst of sinners, Christ Jesus might display his immense patience as an example for those who would believe in him and receive eternal life.

1 TIMOTHY 1:12–16 NIV

After his repentance and spiritual rebirth, God used Paul as the apostle to the Gentiles and to give us two thirds of the New Testament.

Actually, it seems that many well-known people from Scripture, including several in the lineage of Jesus himself, had done things that expressly contradict God's commandments – episodes that were doubtless excruciatingly painful, anxiety-filled and shame-ridden. And yet God continued to love them and use them for an eternal purpose. Because it was never about whether *we* are worthy. It has always been about the fact that *he* is worthy.

Please don't take this to mean that I think what you have done, or what has been done to you, isn't a big deal. That it doesn't hurt or hasn't unalterably changed your life forever. That the shame or guilt or pain isn't crushing. That it wasn't wrong. Or, perhaps whatever you're struggling with isn't something you would call 'massive', and you are just looking for a little extra help or direction, tired of trying to do it all on your own.

Paul didn't deny his struggles, because to deny them would have been to take away from the glory of the God who forgave him and set him free to live out a new life and purpose. This filled him with gratitude, which was at the core of his motivation to do something meaningful with the freedom he found.

Shame will not make the problem go away. Holding grudges and resentment will not protect us. Ignoring our struggles or pain will not bring us peace. What then, can help us? Consider this passage:

> *How blessed is the one whose rebellious acts are forgiven,*
> *whose sin is pardoned!*
> *How blessed is the one whose wrongdoing the* LORD *does*
> *not punish,*
> *in whose spirit there is no deceit.*
> *When I refused to confess my sin,*
> *my whole body wasted away,*
> *while I groaned in pain all day long.*
> *For day and night you tormented me;*
> *you tried to destroy me in the intense heat of summer.*
> *Then I confessed my sin;*
> *I no longer covered up my wrongdoing.*
> *I said, 'I will confess my rebellious acts to the* LORD.'
> *And then you forgave my sins.*
> *For this reason every one of your faithful followers should*
> *pray to you*

while there is a window of opportunity.
Certainly when the surging water rises,
it will not reach them.
You are my hiding place;
you protect me from distress.
You surround me with shouts of joy from those celebrating
deliverance.

PSALM 32:1–7

David, who penned this Psalm, wrestled with horrible guilt after what he had done to Uriah, Bathsheba and his new-born son; but there was one thing he still knew: God loved him. This was where his value was, and he knew he could never lose it. This is what gave him the confidence to admit his problem, repent of his mistakes and cry out to God for help.

Later in David's life, likely after a lifetime of excruciatingly painful experiences, he wrote one of the most well-known psalms in Scripture:

The LORD is my shepherd,
I lack nothing.
He takes me to lush pastures,
he leads me to refreshing water.
He restores my strength.
He leads me down the right paths
for the sake of his reputation.
Even when I must walk through the darkest valley,
I fear no danger,
for you are with me;
your rod and your staff reassure me.
You prepare a feast before me
in plain sight of my enemies.
You refresh my head with oil;
my cup is completely full.

*Surely your goodness and faithfulness will pursue me all
my days,
and I will live in the LORD's house for the rest of my life.*

PSALM 23

How can David say he lacks nothing or that the Lord is leading him beside still waters and lush pastures? How can he have no fear when he has been attacked and hunted and seen so much death and violence?

The answer is that David had made the decision not to focus on his circumstances, but on the things that he believed to be true. That there was a God who loved him, had a plan for him and would never leave him. And that one way or another, God was working it out. And he believed this to such an extent that it gave him peace and hope even in the midst of the most intense conflict and greatest pain of his life.

When I read Psalm 23 in the context of all the things in David's life that seemed so violently out of control, I have to wonder if, in some ways, this psalm is a proclamation of belief in the promises of God despite, or in the face of, his circumstances. It's as if David is proclaiming his belief in the midst of, in defiance against, the whirlwind of circumstances he refuses to allow to define him.

Mike

By this time, my life had totally unravelled, and I was exhausted. I was ready to give up. I remember sitting on the side of my bed looking out the window when I got this thought that I should end it all. I had a small .22 pistol in the top drawer of my chest. There was also a small clip of bullets that I kept in the second drawer. With the kids around, I always kept them separate. I got the gun and sat back on the bed. I got back up and looked in the second drawer but could not find the clip. I looked everywhere, but it was gone. I sat back on the bed, and an image of me looking up from the grave at my three heart-broken daughters at my funeral made me stop what I was doing. By the way, the next time I saw that chest was after we had moved. I opened the second drawer, and that clip was right there in plain sight. Now some can say that was a coincidence, but to me that was a miracle.

At that time, I knew I needed help.

The catalyst for Mike's process of transformation was the recognition that his way of dealing with things just wasn't working. This opened him up to becoming one of 'those' people who met in confidential environments and spoke openly of their problems and struggles with others. It was then that he found the relational network, information and support he needed to make changes. And, in time, this inspired a new sense of purpose in him.

Knowing him, I can tell you that he has helped many men find a new sense of security, significance and freedom in their lives and faith. Far from limiting his service, it was his past struggles, and his honesty and vulnerability about them, that connected him with the community he serves, and became the credentials that kick-started his ministry.

Whatever we have gone through, or are going through, rest assured that God can use it if we let him. We can start the process by praying something like, 'God, I've tried dealing with this on my own. It's not working. I'm ready to turn it over to you and do this your way. If it is your will, please change it supernaturally. But if this is a process you are allowing me to go through for reasons I don't understand right now, then please help me walk this path. Whatever the outcome, whatever the danger, I will trust in your strength to guide me. And I will trust that somehow, some way, you are using even this for good.'

WRITE AND REFLECT

Is there a specific challenge or struggle you can keep in mind as you work through the remainder of this book?

What steps have you taken to work through this in the past?

CHAPTER 5
HISTORY

Alexa

Fast forward to when I was about twelve. We moved to a new town. By this time, I had accepted that I had no value whatsoever to my Dad, so I gave up trying to win his approval. Since I did not feel love from him, I looked elsewhere. Because I was having such a hard time making friends at this new school, I decided I would do whatever it took to get their attention. I did not feel confident, cute or smart, and we were not wealthy, so I had to resort to other measures. I became the most rebellious, daredevil teenager. I would do anything that anyone dared me to do. I would say anything the popular girls wanted me to say to anybody, not caring who it would hurt. I would steal things from shops if they asked me to. I would steal plants off little old lady's porches at night as a dare. Anything. I did not care because it got me the attention that I was starving to death for. I knew in my heart it was wrong and that it saddened God, but I hadn't been close to him in a while anyway. Because I was sure I was unlovable to him too. I couldn't be what my Dad wanted so I was sure I couldn't be what God wanted either.

Let's briefly review what we have covered so far:

1.   No matter who you are, where you've been or what you believe, you were made in God's image. Entangled in past hurts, coping mechanisms and mistakes, that image is still there. Because of that, you have inherent value, and nothing can ever take it away. You are worth dying for. This is the foundation that you can build on and move forward from with confidence.

2.   On top of that, if you are a follower of Christ then you are also a child of God. Forgiven. Redeemed. This identity and destiny are also secure, no matter what. You might try to walk away from him, but you won't shake him. He will pursue you all your life. He doesn't lose anyone who has been given to him. No sin is greater than the cross. Not yours or anyone else's. He has given you hope and a future. He has good plans for you.

3.   And yet, despite this, we all have areas of our lives that don't look the way we'd like. You may have tried to deal with it on your own, doing things that seemed right to you in order to take care of it. But, for whatever reason, it hasn't worked. It would be reasonable to conclude at this point, having tried everything you know, that you are powerless over this difficulty, adversity, struggle or challenge.

4.   However, though you are weak, he is strong. Your willingness to admit you are powerless opens you up to a different way of handling your challenges or struggles – his way.

This new orientation to life's difficulties will lead you into doing things that may at first seem risky or even silly. You may feel vulnerable as you begin to name the things you struggle with. This part of you may feel like a creature that has hidden under a rock its whole life, stepping out into the light for the first time, exposed and looking ... well, like it's been living under a rock. Yet coming out of hiding is your only chance at being found and fully known.

WRITE YOUR OWN STORY

Believing these things, I now encourage you to become brutally honest with yourself – not just about the issue you are dealing with, but also about the context of the issue. This is your life history.

In the pages ahead, you'll document various parts of your life that may be contributing to the difficulty of dealing with this issue in your life. Making it more resistant to change. We'll call this your Personal History Journal.

For example, the person who has a challenging time forgiving their spouse in the present may have forgiven a significant person in their past, only to be hurt again. Once that old wound is uncovered, it can be tended to in the context of a relationship with someone who can empathize with their plight. Then perhaps it can help them explore the difference between that situation and this one, forgiveness and reconciliation, the role of amends, boundaries in relationships and skilful communication – all topics and concepts that we will explore together in the pages ahead. Once that is done, the person may become more willing to explore forgiveness in the present relationship and find freedom from anger, bitterness and resentment.

Going through the Personal History Journal can help you better understand yourself and strengthen the bond you have with God. You can trust him with the details of your life because he already knows them. He will never stop loving you, never condemn or reject you.

It is important to note that the purpose of exploring the past is only to better understand past events and relationships, and how their influence continues to layer itself into present reality.

It's not to blame or scapegoat, or to take on a victim mentality. Once you better understand the impact of the past, you can bring it to the Lord and decide what to do about it in the present.

Ask him if this is the time that he has appointed to review your past and see how it is connected to your present. No doubt there are areas of your life that you do not feel comfortable thinking about, much less writing about. It's also possible that there are certain past experiences that God might not be calling you to revisit. Or, perhaps this is a time for fresh insights, shining a light into what is dark or dim, and a new phase of release and transformation.

WRITE YOUR OWN STORY

Consider the words of Solomon:

> *There is a time for everything,*
> *and a season for every activity under the heavens:*
>
> *a time to be born and a time to die,*
> *a time to plant and a time to uproot,*
> *a time to kill and a time to heal,*
> *a time to tear down and a time to build,*
> *a time to weep and a time to laugh,*
> *a time to mourn and a time to dance,*
> *a time to scatter stones and a time to gather them,*
> *a time to embrace and a time to refrain from embracing,*
> *a time to search and a time to give up,*
> *a time to keep and a time to throw away,*
> *a time to tear and a time to mend,*
> *a time to be silent and a time to speak,*
> *a time to love and a time to hate,*
> *a time for war and a time for peace.*
> ECCLESIASTES 3:1–8 NIV

What would the Lord have you explore or re-visit at this point and time in your life? Even if you have not yet fully put your trust in him, it is entirely possible that he may be wanting to reveal things to you about him and yourself through this exercise.

If you do indeed feel called to this process but are feeling some trepidation, consider what Mary did for Jesus on the week that he was crucified:

> *While he was in Bethany, reclining at the table in the home of Simon the Leper, a woman came with an alabaster jar of very expensive perfume, made of pure nard. She broke the jar and poured the perfume on his head.*
>
> *Some of those present were saying indignantly to one another, 'Why this waste of perfume? It could have been sold for more than a year's wages and the money given to the poor.' And they rebuked her harshly.*
>
> *'Leave her alone,' said Jesus. 'Why are you bothering her? She has done a beautiful thing to me. The poor you will always have with you, and you can help them any time you want. But you will not always have me. She did what she could. She poured perfume on my body beforehand to prepare for my burial. Truly I tell you, wherever the gospel is preached throughout the world, what she has done will also be told, in memory of her.'*

MARK 14:3–9 NIV

Mary took what she had, the thing that was most priceless to her, perhaps what she had all of her security in, and poured it out for Jesus as an act of worship. There would certainly have been a worldly practicality to keeping the nard, which one of the disciples was quick to point out (possibly Judas). Yet Jesus called it *beautiful*.

Why? I don't think it was because it was a lavish gift. Jesus isn't concerned with how much we spend on him. I think it was because Mary did something that revealed her heart to him. It demonstrated that, after seeing all the miracles he did, listening to him teach, seeing his kindness and compassion on so many occasions over the three years of his ministry, Mary *got it*. Though the other (male) disciples still hadn't quite figured it out, she did. She knew who he was: the Messiah. The King. Her Saviour and Redeemer. It was counter-intuitive, counter-cultural; yet in that moment she stopped placing her trust in worldly things that she had a sense of control over – like her life savings – and started placing them instead in Jesus.

We often hold our past, our secrets and our pain quite tightly. We have practical reasons for doing so. I'm not saying it's wrong, just as it would not necessarily have been wrong for Mary to sell her perfume and give the money to the poor. But it would be *beautiful* to smash our pretence, masks and excuses at the feet of Jesus. To be transparent before him and offer him what we have, because we can trust that he is worthy and because we get it like Mary got it. Because we understand that the things we hold so tightly can't save us, and don't guarantee our future. But he does. Whatever we let go, he can replace. Whatever people take from us, he can restore. Whatever doors shut, he can open or lead us to new ones.

WRITE YOUR STORY

Writing your story is an important step in this process, and that is what I will ask you to do in the pages ahead. Something happens when you put pen to paper and begin to write. Connections are made, insights come to the forefront, the Holy Spirit speaks and guides your hand. It can be difficult. It may bring up painful memories. However, it can be beneficial to bring our entanglements, everything that is sedimented within us, into the light of relationship with God and someone we trust so that we can better examine ourselves.

I encourage you to write your history to document the people, places and things that have had an influence on your life and development. No one ever has to see it. In fact, I encourage you to write it like they *won't* see it. Whether they do or not is totally up to you.

This is the creature crawling out from under the rock, blinking in the light, being named and put on a leash for the first time. Or perhaps, set loose.

You can do it. God will help.

PERSONAL HISTORY JOURNAL

Search me, God, and know my heart;
test me and know my anxious thoughts.

PSALM 139:23 NIV

WRITE AND REFLECT

The Issue

What areas of pain, difficulty or challenge exist in your life?

How long has this been going on?

What have you tried so far to address them?

What has worked? What did you like about it?

What hasn't worked? What did you dislike about it?

How would you like to see this issue turn out?

If it turns out the way you hope, what new observable behaviours will you start doing?

If it turns out the way you hope, what observable behaviours will you stop doing?

Significant Relationships

Are your parents divorced/married/re-married/never married? How did/does your parents' relationship status affect you?

What was/is your relationship like with your parents? Were they physically or verbally affectionate? Did they tell you they loved you, hug you, etc.?

How did your parents do discipline? What was that like for you?

How did your parents handle conflict with one another? How did this affect you?

Do you have siblings? If so, please list names, ages, and how you would characterize your relationship.

Does anyone in your family, now or growing up, have any mental health or substance abuse issues that may have affected you?

Does anyone in your family, now or growing up, have any sort of medical or psychological condition that affects you currently, or that affected you as you grew up? (Examples: a parent debilitated with depression, a chronically ill sibling, having to give insulin shots, care for a disabled family member, etc.) If you can think of any situation like this, please describe it and the effect it had on you.

Are you single/married/divorced/re-married? If divorced or re-married, what were the circumstances?

Do you have children? What are their names, ages, and how is your relationship with them?

At school were you social, with lots of friends, or more solitary? Please describe.

Do you have close friends now? How would you describe those relationships?

Development and Career

What were the conditions you grew up in? Did you have enough money, food, clothing? Was it safe? Please describe each location you lived at to the age of eighteen.

Please describe your education level and experience.

What is your occupation? What do you like or dislike about it?

What interests or hobbies bring you joy? What do you like about them?

Do you now, or have you in the past, used drugs or alcohol? What kind, how much?

What is your spiritual history?

Did you ever have any anxiety issues as a child around school or friends? Do you currently experience anxiety?

Relational Wounds

Note: Due to the sensitive nature of this section, I strongly suggest you write it in a separate document that you can keep secure. Remember that it may not be the time to do this kind of work alone. If it feels too difficult, please consider getting additional support.

If you have been hurt by many people, to avoid being overwhelmed you might find it helpful to only focus on a specific part of your life, leaving the rest for processing at another time. If one person or group of people has hurt you the same way repeatedly, you only need list it once and then describe the effect it typically had on you each time.

Who has hurt you in a way you think of as significant? For each hurt, write how you think it affected you at the time when you were hurt.

For each hurt, write how you think it might continue to affect you in the present. Think and pray about how these past hurts might play a role in the issue you listed at the beginning of this journal.

Have you considered forgiving those who have hurt you, or attempted to forgive them? Please describe for each offence. If you have not forgiven them, or not considered it, what are your reasons?

What is the status of each of those relationships today?

Who have you hurt, and how?

Have you made amends or attempted to? Please describe.

What is the status of those relationships today?

Re-assessing the Problem

Keeping what you've journalled about so far in mind, is there anything about your goals for this study that you would like to change? If so, please amend them in the space below.

SHARING YOUR LESSONS

Nancy

I came to LifeCare feeling battered, confused and angry after several adverse life events hit me in just a few months. I was getting treatment for depression at the time. My LifeCarer was kind, practical and didn't expect too much from me. She helped me to identify an area we could work on, although I was doubtful that I could make any progress during such a hard season.

She broke it all down into tiny achievable steps and practiced each step with me so that I could see and report back success almost straight away. Some weeks I was too squashed to attend to business and she patiently listened and supported instead. I never felt judged; I felt she was actively cheerleading me and wanting me to succeed.

As the months went by, I found myself applying what I had learned in different life settings. The principles work really well. It's exciting to see how I can now do what seemed so difficult at the beginning. Many of the stressful situations remain but my future looks manageable and I'm back in control. My confidence has grown a lot and I can keep using the principles from now on.

CONGRATULATIONS!

You have taken a big step towards freedom by taking a brutally honest look at your past, and how it may be affecting you in the present. We can't change our past, but we can change the way we think about it, what we will do about it and what we will do from this point forward to address it.

Also, there may be clues in your past about your life purpose – things you might be passionate about. Perhaps you're called to help others overcome the same things you've experienced or are still living through. Who better to empathize with and understand them than you?

In the beginning of this exercise I asked you to write your answers like you were never going to share them with anyone. And you don't ever have to. So, take a breath, praise God and celebrate the progress you've made so far. Really, well done!

If you're feeling pretty rough after going through all that, that's OK. It's normal. It may not feel good now, but we're not going to leave you there. Remember that no emotion lasts forever. We will get through this together in the pages ahead.

And, if you want, now that you are aware of these issues, know that it is OK to set them aside for a while. Go do something else. Let your attention go elsewhere. All this will be here when you are ready to come back to it. You're not in denial or trying to escape, you're just recharging your batteries.

When you are ready, the next big step will be to consider sharing what you have learned through this process with someone else. Why do this? Why share with others what has been difficult to even admit to yourself? One reason, commonly known and shared in recovery circles, is: 'You're as sick as your secrets'.

Secrets keep us in bondage. The enemy uses them to tell us that if anyone knew, they would condemn us. He wants us to believe that if people saw us as we really were, they would get sick and run screaming from the room. That when the creature crawled out from under the rock, it would inspire revulsion and either be abandoned or hunted.

I want to tell you that's not possible. But unfortunately, it is. Some people will judge, condemn and reject you. Most likely, you have already experienced this at some point in your life. Sadly, and surely something we all grieve on some level, is the fact that not all people are safe, and it is important to determine who is and isn't safe to talk to about the most sensitive areas of your life. We will talk more about this when we come to the section on shame and guilt.

Until then, it is important to remember first and foremost that, as a follower of Christ, you have been forgiven, redeemed, are worth enough to die for and he will never judge you or leave you. Second, it is important for you to know that he wants to give you an experience of his grace by connecting you to someone you *can* trust, who will respond to you with his grace and love, rather than judgment or condemnation. When you experience this with one person, you can begin to believe that other people might actually love and accept you too, despite your flaws, just like God does. It is at this point that your secrets begin to lose their power over you. The shame goes away. The guilt is dealt with.

It's one thing to read about God's grace in Scripture, and quite another to allow someone else to be the hands and feet of Jesus; someone who can listen, encourage, pray for and love you in a healthy way as you share your story.

This concept resonates with the work of neuropsychologist Dr Curt Thompson, who writes,

> ... it is only through this process of being known that you come to know yourself and learn how to know others. There is no other way. To be known is to be pursued, examined, and shaken. To be known is to be loved and to have hopes and even demands placed upon you ... To be known, means that you allow your shame and guilt to be exposed – in order for them to be healed.[15]

That is why I encourage you to connect with a trusted mentor, counsellor or friend to share your history. It's not to make you do something hard. It's to encourage you to do something that allows you to become truly known, so that you can experience what it is like to be truly loved and accepted. All of you. Not just the nice-looking parts.

Alternatively, consider enrolling in LifeCare Training. There you will have the opportunity to share as much of your history as you would like with a fellow LifeCare trainee who, like you, is seeking greater 'response-ability' in relationship to their entanglements, so that they might be used by God as an instrument to help others do the same. Even in the training, you will have the

---

15 Thompson, *Anatomy of the Soul*, p.21.

opportunity to be Jesus to someone else who shares their history with you.

Please read, and really absorb, the words of Paul in his second letter to the Corinthians:

Blessed is the God and Father of our Lord Jesus Christ, the Father of mercies and God of all comfort, who comforts us in all our troubles so that we may be able to comfort those experiencing any trouble with the comfort with which we ourselves are comforted by God. For just as the sufferings of Christ overflow toward us, so also our comfort through Christ overflows to you. But if we are afflicted, it is for your comfort and salvation; if we are comforted, it is for your comfort that you experience in your patient endurance of the same sufferings that we also suffer. And our hope for you is steadfast because we know that as you share in our sufferings, so also you will share our comfort.

2 CORINTHIANS 1:3-7

I strongly encourage you to experience what it is like to be fully known and accepted by another, and to have the honour of giving that experience to someone else. God bless you and keep you in this process with him, knowing with full confidence that he loves you, is for you and has great plans for your life.

Alexa

It was by sorting through my past with the ladies in my group that I could see where my current struggles started to develop. For example, on one occasion, my sisters and I were told to pick up and tidy away all of our toys in the store room or my Daddy was going to burn them all. So when we came in from school we worked and worked doing just that. We thought he would be pleased with us, but when he came home from work and came out to the store room, he started yelling and cursing. He was furious because he said we did not do what he had told us to do. He gathered up all our toys that we had arranged so neatly and dumped them in the burning barrel, poured gas on them and burnt them all! We were horrified because we thought we had done so good. I was about five years old then, but it left a huge impression. Once again, I thought something must be wrong with me to think we had done so good, for it to have turned out so badly.

Birdie

When I share – and people love me enough to not judge me and respect my feelings enough to just let me have them – and trust God to fix me so they don't have to, he always does.

CHAPTER 6

DISENTANGLING OUR IDENTITY

Malik

I wrote down all the things I had done to hurt others and the things they had done to hurt me. I confessed all this to my brother. After I did that, I knew in my heart I needed to confess to my wife but I didn't want to 'hurt' her by making amends, so I decided I would just change without 'hurting' her by confessing.

But then, later, I saw a testimony from someone at church. I don't even remember what it was, but I was so shame-filled and convicted that I decided I needed to confess right now. I told my brother that there would be big issues coming up and they may have to watch the kids, or I might have to stay at his house. I was not sure what would happen. I knew one thing for sure. I decided at that moment to give up, I was not going to fight God anymore and I was going to do what he said to do.

I died right then and started as a new man. That new man informed his wife that we were going to miss our appointment at the Apple Store; I had something I wanted to talk about. I confessed all the sins to the best of my memory right then in the parking lot of the church. I was tired of the addiction and insanity of my life. I knew that tough days were ahead, and I was afraid. I had to face my greatest fears, to live life in the opposite direction.

I dived in; I decided that all the questioning and all the fighting regarding Christ no longer mattered. His pathway would be my one and only pathway. My ways led me to resentment, anger, bitterness and disappointment and I knew it. I was broken, I was ready to die and let him live in me instead.

If you have worked through the Personal History Journal, it will have helped you gain a great deal of insight into entanglements that contribute to the way you act, feel and think. If you have shared your story with another person, you now have an ally with whom you can face current life challenges.

Fortified by your new insights, your ally, and your knowledge about what God says is your true identity, it is time to live – that is: to act, feel and think – as if these things were actually true. You are now going to align your day-to-day choices with what you say you believe:

- If it is true that you have value no matter what, then you are going to act as if you have value in every situation.
- If it is true that you were made for a purpose, then you are going to discover that purpose and begin pursuing it.
- If it is true that you are already redeemed, then by faith you are going to behave as though you have confidence and are free from shame.
- If it is true that you are safe with Christ in this life and the next, then you are going to begin to confront what you have been afraid of in the past.
- If it is true that you are loved, then you are going to build relationships knowing that you are worthy of love.

In the beginning, though you accept these truths in your head, you may have a hard time feeling as though they are true. That's normal, and something we can work on. It will take time to overcome the negative messages of the past, but it is possible. Remember, under all the mistakes and pain, you are foundationally strong.

Jesus is inviting you to believe that you are what he says you are, and to accept your God-given identity in him – not as something you have earned, but as a free gift. Perhaps this is at least part of what he meant when he said,

> *'Come to me, all you who are weary and burdened, and I will give you rest. Take my yoke on you and learn from me, because I am gentle and humble in heart, and you will find rest for your souls. For my yoke is easy to bear, and my load is not hard to carry.'*

MATTHEW 11:28–30

To take on the yoke of Jesus is to agree that we belong to him, that we are valued, and that we can rest in his guidance and provision to plough the fields he leads us to.

'Sounds great,' you say. 'But how do I do that?'

The first step is to do a diagnostic exercise that will help you identify where exactly your head and heart are disconnected when it comes to God's word about you. Read the 'Letter from the Lord' on the next page, which is a collection of God's promises and proclamations from Scripture, crafted into a personal letter from God to you. It is important to note that this 'letter' is not Scripture in and of itself. It does however, seek to represent Scripture accurately and each citation is clearly included so you can check the statements against the corresponding verse in the Bible.

Read it aloud. Take your time. Envision that this letter really was written to you, really is meant for you specifically.

As you read, you may notice that certain parts of the letter evoke some emotion in you. There could be many reasons for this. One is simple gratitude for the goodness and love of

Christ. Or perhaps this is because, as much as you believe these truths cognitively, you don't feel them to be true. This might be because the words speak to some aspect of your upbringing, or don't seem to fit with certain experiences you've been through. Another reason might just be that you've never heard these things before – you didn't know that God loved you in such a personal, relational way – and something in your heart is responding to God's message of forgiveness and restoration.

Whatever the case, as you read, make a note of the parts of the letter that mean the most to you, or evoke emotion in you. Be specific about why they are so personal for you. What have you experienced that doesn't seem to match the promises of God? What have you been told by others that Scripture is challenging in these verses?

When you are finished, record your responses in the space at the end of this chapter.

Dear Child,

I'm writing because I know that, sometimes, you have questions about life (Psalm 139:1). I know this because I know everything about you (1 John 3:20). I know every pain, disappointment and unmet need; and not just in you either, but in your parents and their parents – all the way back (1 Kings 8:39). Because of all that, I understand what you're going through and why (Hebrews 4:13–15).

So, I want to tell you a few things that might help, though I know it will still be hard for you – it was hard for me too (Hebrews 2:10).

Firstly, I made you in my image (Genesis 1:27). Secondly, you are worth so much to me that I was willing to die so that we might have a relationship (Romans 5:6–8). Thirdly, I knit you together in a very special way (Psalm 139:13). Those three things alone should tell you that you are incredibly valuable, and nothing can ever take that away (Romans 8:38–39).

I didn't cause the evil you've experienced (Deuteronomy 32:4). That comes from a fallen world (1 John 2:15–17), filled with fallen people (James 1:13–15), and an enemy that seeks to destroy you (1 Peter 5:8–10) because he knows I love you, and he wants to try and separate us (Genesis 3:1). He is relentless and cunning (2 Corinthians 11:3) – watch out for him.

I know you can't fully understand certain things and you might be angry, hurt or confused at times (Job 3). But I am asking you to trust me (Job 42:3). I promise I will use it all for good if you'll let me (Romans 8:28). Sometimes you'll see this happen in your lifetime, and sometimes it will take generations (Acts 3:17–21). But I promise you that if you do trust me, it will all be worth it – you'll see (2 Corinthians 4:17-18).

In the meantime, you need to know that I have a plan and a purpose for your life (Jeremiah 29:11). I have given you gifts and abilities to do what I created you to do (Jeremiah 1:5). I will guide you by my word and Spirit into these things (John 16:13). Do your best to listen to my voice and follow me (John 10:27–28).

I know things were not perfect where you were born (Genesis 25) – sometimes far from it (Genesis 38). Sometimes it was really bad (Genesis 19). Please remember that's not how I designed the world to be (Genesis 1:31) and that I never left your side (Psalm 23). There will be justice – you can trust me for that (Ecclesiastes 12:14). Justice is part of who I am (Psalm 7:11–12). You need to know that when injustice grieves you it grieves me even more, and something will be done about it – just leave it with me (Revelation 15:3).

At the same time, you never have to be ashamed around me for your mistakes and failures (Romans 5:5). My son, Jesus, paid for those on the cross for everyone who believes in him (Romans 5:1-2). I am the Father who will always love you, no matter what (Psalm 13:5). I am so for you (Romans 8:31)! In good times and bad, when you are doing well and when you are struggling (Jeremiah 31:3). Even if you run in the opposite direction to me (Luke 15), I will still be with you (Psalm 139:7). Even when there are consequences for your mistakes (Galatians 6:7), I will not abandon you (Deuteronomy 31:6).

Don't ever let anyone tell you different – remember that Satan is a liar and the father of lies (John 8:44), and that is so often how he likes to attack. Fight his lies with the truth of my word (Ephesians 4:12-17).

The world is not an easy place to live in but hang on (Psalm 116:1-12). I do have good things for you (Matthew 7:11). I absolutely delight in giving them to you (Zephaniah 3:17). One is your unique purpose and mission (Ephesians 2:10) – I will even reward you for using the gifts I give you to do your mission (Col 3:23-24)! Another is the hope you have in eternity, where there's no more sadness and you'll experience more and more of my love forever (Luke 6:20).

You might have a hard time seeing me in the situations you'll face as you do the work I have for you (2 Corinthians 6:1-10). But you can be sure that I am with you (Matthew 28:20). If you seek me, you will find me (Matthew 7:7). I will light your path (Psalm 119:105).

Remember, you are always in my thoughts and you always will be (Psalm 139:17-18).

With love

Dad

WRITE AND REFLECT

Personal Application

What encourages you about God's promises in this letter?

Which verses brought up some emotion in you?

What experiences have you had that seem to affirm these truths?

What experiences have you had that lead you to question, or even have a hard time *feeling,* that these verses are true?

This exercise is a good reminder of things that God has promised you and that the enemy has actively been trying to steal. And it seems that something about the process of reclaiming them is important to God. One major indication of this is that he went through it himself. He didn't stay insulated from the pain of this world and forgive us from a distance. That would have been too relationally disconnected. Nor did he turn a blind eye to the ways in which we've hurt one another and redeem us anyway. That wouldn't be justice. Since God is perfectly just, and since he is Immanuel (God with us), he couldn't do either of those things without violating his own nature.

Instead, he maintained his perfect standard of justice and relationship, which required that a penalty be paid, and then he paid it himself while in relationship with others as a son, brother, teacher and friend. Through that process, the sins of the world were forgiven ... and something else happened that is hard to make sense of. Somehow through the process of paying our debts, Jesus, who was already perfect, is said to have been *perfected* (Hebrews 2:10). No one is really, completely sure how that works (how do you perfect the perfect?) but it seems safe to say that somehow, something about the process Christ went through mattered.

Regardless of your situation, because the world keeps coming, the enemy keeps coming and there are always new challenges and higher goals to aim for, we are often faced with new trials and tribulations. We don't just learn these things once. We learn them again and again, each time in new and deeper ways as our faith grows in depth and breadth of experience and our lives continue to unfold.

When Jesus returns, things will be different. Until then, we have some work to do as we allow the Holy Spirit to guide us into all truth (John 16:13) so that we might continue sharing his message of love and grace to a hurting world in whatever ways he calls us to.

OPTIONAL EXERCISE

Consider sharing your answers with the person you chose to share your Personal History Journal with.

If you are not yet comfortable at this stage sharing your feelings about these verses with others, I encourage you to journal and pray about them. Remember that, when you're ready, you can choose to reach out to a trusted pastor, counsellor, friend, mentor or recovery partner to share what you have discovered.

Moving Ahead

Your responses to the 'Letter from the Lord' can give you clues about distortions in your thinking or lies you may believe about yourself regarding who and what you are. Connecting these lies or distortions to your responses in the Personal History Journal can help you begin to understand why you were susceptible to this unhelpful way of thinking or believing. And, now that we have exposed these potentially unhelpful or untrue thoughts and beliefs, the next step will be to begin challenging them and changing them. Your goal will be to take them captive and make them align with what God says about you, and with his promises (2 Corinthians 10:5).

In the next two chapters, we will be discussing strategies to change thoughts, feelings and behaviours. As you will see, they are all connected to one another. A change in one can begin to change the others.

For example, doing a fun activity, even when you don't feel like it, can change your emotions and thinking patterns. Similarly, changing your thinking about something can lead to changes in behaviours and emotions.

Chapter 7 will focus on strategies to help you change your thinking, which will lead to changes in your behaviours and emotions. Chapter 8 will focus on ways to change your behaviours in order to change your emotions and thinking.

Different strategies will work better for different people and in different contexts. It is up to you to decide what works best for you and when.

CHAPTER 7

INTERPRETATIONS & WORLDVIEW

Laura

I think I was unprepared for many things that would begin to happen in my forties. Hardest of all was that parenting began to become very unpredictable. Control freaks never notice they're control freaks until they begin to lose control. My oldest child began hitting the normal bumps of adolescence and this was hard for me. He began to push away from me, and secretly I really believed this only happened to everyone else, not me. I now know this is normal and even a good thing for a son. But at the time, it really hurt. He had ups and downs in life and school, and I felt them as if they were happening to me. I began to really invest myself in making sure he looked good on the outside. After all, this was my specialty and I was looking very nice, so I began to try and make sure he was too. My spiritual life became dry and stale. I was tired and discouraged. I couldn't just make it all better for him and this frustrated me. I started to hear a voice in my ear say, 'This is as good as it's ever going to get.'

I have since come to change the way I think about these things. I know now that I cannot control outcomes for my family, or myself, but I can rest in the one who has all the answers. Psalm 27:1 says:

> *The LORD is my light and my salvation –*
> *Whom shall I fear?*
> *The LORD is the stronghold of my life –*
> *Of whom shall I be afraid?* NIV

He truly is my only solution.

That image I worked so hard on for years, trying to manage what others thought of me, seems so unimportant now when I compare it to being truly free. To lay my head on my pillow at night and know that I have no secrets! Life weighs a lot less than it used to.

CHANGING HOW YOU THINK

Laura changed the way she thought about her image, and who she was at her foundation – regardless of what others thought about her.

It is possible for you, too, to change the way you think about something, which can then change the way you act and feel – even the way your body feels ... for example, butterflies in your stomach, shakiness, dry mouth or a sinking feeling in your gut. In fact, your brain comes equipped with some significant features that support this type of change. If you're interested in reading more about the research-based links that have been made between changing our thoughts, feelings and beliefs, I've included several studies in Appendix 2. There's much more material out there as this is a well-researched topic, but this will get you started.

LINKS

Not only are thoughts and behaviours linked to your feelings and beliefs, they are also points of intra-connection with the world around you. What others do to and around us will generate arousal, fear, anger or happiness. We interpret these experiences in order to make sense of them. What others say to us also shapes our belief system and sense of identity, which form our *worldview* – how we see the world around us and ourselves in relationship to it. These points of intra-connection are constantly buzzing with activity as we intra-act with people and our environment.

Thousands of years before this research was done, links between behaviours, emotions, thoughts and physiological states could be found in Scripture. Let's review some of them before we talk about how to use these hard-wired dynamics to our advantage in daily life.

> *Therefore, I urge you, brothers and sisters, in view of God's mercy, to offer your bodies as a living sacrifice, holy and pleasing to God – this is your true and proper worship. Do not conform to the pattern of this world, but be transformed by the renewing of your mind. Then you will be able to test and approve what God's will is – his good, pleasing and perfect will.*

ROMANS 12:1–2 NIV

I doubt that Paul understood the neuropsychological concept that we could be transformed by the literal renewing of our minds by changing our brain's physical structure through selective focus, but our Creator certainly did. These verses urge us to focus on God's mercy (thoughts) which then leads to a transformation of mind, brain and behaviour, leading in turn to the experiential understanding that God's will is good and pleasing for us.

This is why, throughout Scripture, the Lord stresses the importance of knowing, understanding and memorizing his word. For example:

> *Hear, O Israel: The LORD our God, the LORD is one. Love the LORD your God with all your heart and with all your soul and with all your strength. These commandments that I give you today are to be on your hearts. Impress them on your*

children. Talk about them when you sit at home and when you walk along the road, when you lie down and when you get up. Tie them as symbols on your hands and bind them on your foreheads. Write them on the door-frames of your houses and on your gates.

DEUTERONOMY 6:4–9 NIV

This prayer is known as the *Shema* (Hebrew for the first word of the prayer, 'hear'), which was the most important Jewish prayer in the Old Testament period. It emphasizes the connection between beliefs about the nature of God, love for God and his commandments to the Israelites. The believing and focusing were essential to the behavioural following of the commandments.

In fact, regarding Hebrew philosophy, Thrall and company write:

Hebrews did not separate the heart from the mind, or belief from action. They were one and the same. What you believed affected all you did, from cooking a meal to building a city. What you did reflected what you believed.

ASCENT OF A LEADER[16]

Jesus upheld the importance of the *Shema* for believers today. An incident is recorded in Mark 12 where Jesus was asked what the most important commandment was. Notice again the link between beliefs and actions in his reply. The Greek word used for loving one's neighbour here is *ag-ap-ah'-o* which implies action, not just feeling.

Now one of the experts in the law came and heard them debating. When he saw that Jesus answered them well, he asked him, 'Which commandment is the most important of all?' Jesus answered, 'The most important is: "Listen, Israel, the Lord our God, the Lord is one. Love the Lord your

16 Thrall, McNicol, McElrath, *Ascent of a Leader*, pp.101-102.

God with all your heart, with all your soul, with all your mind, and with all your strength." The second is: "Love your neighbour as yourself." There is no other commandment greater than these.'

MARK 12:28–31

We are to love God and our neighbour, but we are also to do something about it. It is our action, based on our love for God and others, that bridges the gap between the sanctification happening *in* us, and the expression of kingdom values that happens *through* us.

In the verse below, we see Paul, a 'Hebrew of Hebrews' according to his own testimony in Philippians 3:5, once again connecting what we choose to focus on and believe to be true with godly behaviour and peace.

Finally, brothers and sisters, whatever is true, whatever is noble, whatever is right, whatever is pure, whatever is lovely, whatever is admirable – if anything is excellent or praiseworthy – think about such things. Whatever you have learned or received or heard from me, or seen in me – put it into practice. And the God of peace will be with you.

PHILIPPIANS 4:8–9 NIV

FEELING AND BELIEVING

Thinking about whatever is lovely, pure and so on, is wonderful. But Paul echoes Jesus' sentiment that feeling and believing are not enough on their own. We must also put what we have learned into practice. That is what leads to peace.

And it is not only neuroscience and the biblical witness that agree on this topic. Various kinds of counselling and psycho-therapy are focused around the idea that emotions, physiological responses and behaviours are connected to our thoughts and beliefs about reality, rather than to reality itself. That is why two people faced with the same situation may have a different interpretation of the situation, and therefore different emotions, physiological responses and behaviours.

Moreover, we are entangled with our physical environment, spiritual beliefs, thoughts and goals in such a way that these forces shape and add definition to us, on a moment-by-moment basis, in the unending liminality of the world (see Chapter 1). This does not mean that these forces are able to erase or supersede what we are at a foundational level, or who we are in relationship to our Saviour. God is the pre-eminent force that shaped us in his image, breathed life into us, knew us while we were still in the womb, saw our lives from beginning to end and thought we were worth dying for. When we accepted Christ as Lord, we became intra-connected with him in a way that overcame sin and death for all eternity. These material and discursive entanglements transcend all others and are as real as any other material or immaterial force.

Nevertheless, what we believe and what we do affect other people and the things and ideas with which they are connected/entangled. These then go on to come into being and affect other things and so on, each 'happening' inextricably entwined with what is, and what will come to be. For these reasons, we will look at strategies to become aware of, and change, our thoughts, emotions and behaviours.

The choice to work on your thought life involves helping you see things from a different perspective and coming up with a way of looking at your situation that helps you change whatever you are willing and able to change. At the least, changing our perspective can help us address the situation more effectively, even when we are truly powerless to change it completely.

It is very important to understand this is meant to be empowering, not shaming. Sometimes, people face horrible situations which are not their fault and that they have no control over. For example, survivors of assault, natural disaster, war, racism, discrimination, disease and so on. If you have experienced any of these things, please know that those were painful events in and of themselves, not just because of the way you think about them.

Although many of us face real and painful situations, and it makes sense that we are hurt, it is up to us how we will choose to think about and respond to what has happened to us.

To use a couple of common examples, some people begin the journey of changing the way they think about painful experiences by rejecting the identity of 'victim' ('I am a victim of _____') and replacing it with that of a 'survivor' ('I am a survivor of _____'). When struggling to learn a new task, telling yourself, 'I can't do it,' can lead to a feeling of hopelessness and inspire you to give up. Telling yourself, 'I can't do it *yet*,' may inspire you to persevere.

At the other end of these experiences are people who have made terrible mistakes that had real consequences for themselves and others, which have lead to crippling guilt and shame. If you have hurt someone badly, I am *not* advocating that you simply change your perspective in an attempt to downplay the impact of what you've done in order to get some relief or dodge responsibility. This is where your personal values will come into play (in Chapter 9 we will discuss the purpose of guilt, which is to let us know when we have violated our own moral beliefs, what to do when that happens and how guilt differs from its more toxic cousin – shame).

However, whilst what we may have done done will certainly affect us and others in many ways, it does not need to become our primary identity, and it does not change what we are at a foundational level. We can choose to change our view of ourselves from that of a bad person, to that of a person who did a bad thing. One is redeemable, while the other isn't. One is something we can learn and grow from, and the other condemns us to a negative identity and low self-worth (a form of shame) that will likely lead us into more painful mistakes in the future.

Changing our perspective doesn't change what we did, or what was done to us, but it can empower us to heal and move forward in life in a more positive and effective way.

For these reasons, we can challenge people when they say that something 'makes' them feel a certain way. We can ask if it is really the situation that is 'making' them feel something, or if it is the way they are thinking about their situation that is 'making them' feel something.

THE ENEMY DISTORTS REALITY

From a spiritual perspective, it is important to remember that we have an enemy who has distorted reality by introducing sin into the world. One of the ways in which we see the impact of sin is through the destructive force of lies and half-truths. These affect the way we think, which inspires destructive actions and feelings. It is important to remember that lies are not from God. Scripture says,

> *All your words are true;*
> *all your righteous laws are eternal.*

PSALM 119:160 NIV

> *Paul, a servant of God and an apostle of Jesus Christ to further the faith of God's elect and their knowledge of the truth that leads to godliness – in the hope of eternal life, which God, who does not lie, promised before the beginning of time ...*

TITUS 1:1–2 NIV

Rather, lies are from the enemy:

You belong to your father, the devil, and you want to carry out your father's desires. He was a murderer from the beginning, not holding to the truth, for there is no truth in him. When he lies, he speaks his native language, for he is a liar and the father of lies.

JOHN 8:44 NIV

The desire of the enemy is to destroy us, but God has given us a way to resist.

Cast all your anxiety on him because he cares for you. Be alert and of sober mind. Your enemy the devil prowls around like a roaring lion looking for someone to devour. Resist him, standing firm in the faith, because you know that the family of believers throughout the world is undergoing the same kind of sufferings.

1 PETER 5:7–9 NIV

But now, put off all such things as anger, rage, malice, slander, abusive language from your mouth. Do not lie to one another since you have put off the old man with its practices and have been clothed with the new man that is being renewed in knowledge according to the image of the one who created it.

COLOSSIANS 3:8–10

We resist and defeat the enemy by being alert, of sober mind and standing firm in the faith when he is trying to attack us with lies. By being sanctified through increasing unity of faith and knowledge of Jesus, resulting in our increasing maturity and likeness to Christ (Ephesians 4:13). This requires us to examine our thought life and make sure we are interpreting the world around us through the lens of our faith, values and goals.

Birdie

I know now *it is the Lord who has always kept me going. He built me strong from birth, he protected me from my stalker, he was my friend when I had no others, he prayed for me when I had no words, he refreshed my faith in him almost constantly even when I wasn't walking with him and he showed himself in the world all around me – in the soft lamb's wool cushion of my ballet pointe shoes, in the wave I floated on near a sandy beach, in the way my mother stroked my hair in the middle of the night, in the love of the Special Olympics team members I coached, in the way my dog kissed me when I was crying, in the freedom of being able to move States or just wherever, in the words of a song and in the gentleness of a boy in a Women's Writing graduate school class who made a point to talk to me in the stairwell during class breaks. That boy persisted in asking me out and became my best friend, and eventually my husband and the father of my four beautiful children: one in heaven and three in my house.*

UNDERSTANDING HOW OUR THOUGHTS AND BELIEFS ARE STRUCTURED

Many people have found it helpful to have a visual illustration that gives them a way to think about how their thoughts, actions and emotions fit together. And of course, people live in a context too, a past and a present life, which you will have explored in the Personal History Journal. All these intra-relating components of life are represented by the diagram of the Jeremiah Tree on page 122.

The Jeremiah Tree consists of the following components:

God-given Foundation – Our inherent value is symbolized here by the roots of the tree growing into the foundation of our faith, which is Christ himself. While all trees have roots, some of them are shallow, and will be easily uprooted when the environment becomes hostile. A tree with shallow roots is like a person whose value and worth rest on their accomplishments and/or the opinions of others. It is only when our connection to what we are is deeply rooted in our knowledge and faith in Christ that we have access to the living water – a bottomless source of purpose and hope, no matter what else might be happening to or around us. We covered this in detail in Chapter 2.

Worldview and Identity – These are symbolized by the trunk of the tree. Our worldview is made up of thoughts and beliefs about how the world works, or ought to work, according to us. It develops through experiences and things we were taught over time. A significant piece of our worldview is who and what we see ourselves to be. There is an intimate relationship between the way we see the world and the way we see ourselves. How we see one shapes how we see the other. They are intra-related (see Chapter 1).

Interpretations – These are symbolized by the branches of the tree. Interpretations are our ongoing thoughts about minute-by-minute experiences in life. We often don't notice them, but they're running in the background, constantly processing and categorizing the millions of pieces of data that are flowing through our senses every day. Our interpretations are supported by the tree trunk (worldview), which in turn is supported by the roots (whether they are quite shallow, or firmly planted in the foundation of your inherent value in Christ).

Adversity, Thoughts, Emotions and Behaviours – These are symbolized by the leaves of the tree. They could include addictions, relationship problems, problematic emotions, etc. How many of the leaves are healthy or unhealthy depends on the health of the tree overall. It could be that the tree is ninety per cent healthy and just has a bad branch or two. Or it could be that the whole tree is infected with lies and distortions, all the way down to the roots.

History and Present Context – This is represented by the soil. The soil includes our past history and our current context. As discussed in Chapter 1, these are important elements that shape the way we grow, develop and live on a daily basis. Knowing what's in our soil, or is not in our soil, is a very important part of understanding ourselves.

Actions and Attitudes – These are symbolized by leaves that fall to the soil, shaping it as they decompose and are absorbed back into the earth. As we live, what we do affects the world around us, including the soil that we and other trees grow in.

Finally, I want to call your attention to the two key verses at the top and bottom of the page.

2 Corinthians 10:5 – This verse is here to remind us that there is an element of life that involves spiritual battle. One of the weapons the enemy uses to attack you is the lie. That is why it is so important to not simply accept your thoughts as always being accurate and true even when they feel true. Rather, examine them and make sure that they reflect your spiritual beliefs and are consistent with your long-term goals. I would even go so far as to say that this is one of the most common, yet unrecognized forms of spiritual warfare you will face in this world.

Jeremiah 17: 7–8 – The diagram gets its name from this verse, which is located at the bottom of the page to remind you that under the soil lies a hidden source of living water (John 4:10–11) that is accessible to anyone who believes in Jesus and accepts him as their Lord. No matter what your circumstances or history, your roots can always tap into it to for perspective, peace and wisdom. To let you know that no matter what you've done, what has been done to you, or what you are currently going through you are loved by God, made in his image and worth enough to die for. To let you know that there is a plan and purpose for your life in his Church, and the gates of hell will not prevail against it (1 Corinthians 12:27, Mathew 16:18). To remind you of God's promise that whatever is not made right in this life will be made right in the next (Revelation 21:4).

The thoughts you process in the pages ahead will be located somewhere on the diagram but will have to do with your tree as a whole. I suggest taking some time to read through and familiarize yourself with the Jeremiah Tree diagram on the next page, so that you might better understand how each area you work on is connected to the others.

As you progress, keep in mind that the deeper the beliefs, the more potentially painful they may be to examine, but the more profitable it may be to change them to something more positive and helpful.

I also want to make sure you understand that these are often difficult skills to master. They are not once-and-done, and it will likely take more than simply reading through this chapter in order to grasp and apply the concepts. It takes repeated practice with them over time to make a difference in your life. In my various roles as a missionary, counsellor and pastor I have met with people in private for many weeks in a row, helping them to learn and apply these concepts. However, I have found that once a person does gain these skills, they keep them forever.

For this reason, I urge you again to consider getting some extra support if you find yourself coming across beliefs or past experiences that are particularly painful. There's no reason for you to struggle alone. The more significant the stress or abuse you have lived through, the more challenging the goals you have set for yourself, the more likely it is that you will benefit from a trained and trusted ally who can work through this programme alongside you and help you progress.

JEREMIAH TREE

We demolish arguments and every pretension that sets itself up against the knowledge of God, and we take captive every thought to make it obedient to Christ.

2 CORINTHIANS 10:5 NIV

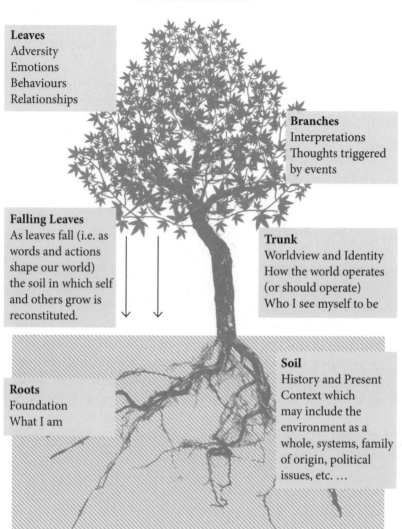

Leaves
Adversity
Emotions
Behaviours
Relationships

Branches
Interpretations
Thoughts triggered
by events

Falling Leaves
As leaves fall (i.e. as
words and actions
shape our world)
the soil in which self
and others grow is
reconstituted.

Trunk
Worldview and Identity
How the world operates
(or should operate)
Who I see myself to be

Roots
Foundation
What I am

Soil
History and Present
Context which
may include the
environment as a
whole, systems, family
of origin, political
issues, etc. …

Water source under the soil

But blessed is the one who trusts in the LORD, whose confidence is in him. They will be like a tree planted by the water that sends out its roots by the stream.

JEREMIAH 17:7-8 NIV

WRITE AND REFLECT

Distressing Thought Form

With this mental map of your thought life and environment as an aid, it is time to begin filling out your tree. You don't need to identify every thought and belief you have – just the ones that are causing you trouble in life. The way to do this is to first learn to identify or target those thoughts that lead to unwanted or unhelpful feelings and behaviours.

To get started, think about a time when you were in your normal state, and then something happened which led to you feeling distressed or doing something that you later came to regret. We'll call this thing that happened a 'trigger', because it activated a distressing thought, feeling and/or behaviour.

Take a moment now to identify a recent event that triggered you. Make a brief note of it in one summary sentence or phrase. What happened? Describe what a camera videoing the event would have picked up, or what someone would have seen if they had been watching you.

Next, try to recall what you thought in response to the triggering event. Try to focus on one single thought that popped into your head right then in the moment that you were triggered. What was the thought?

After you had that thought, how did you feel right then in that moment? Try to use a 'feeling' word such as happy, sad, mad or glad. What did you feel?

Now, what did you actually do right then in that moment after you thought what you thought, and felt what you felt? What did you do?

Finally, how were you feeling going into this situation, generally speaking? Were you tired, stressed, hurt, angry? These are 'vulnerability factors' that may have made you more likely to respond in a way that wasn't helpful to the trigger event.

By reviewing the answers above, you may begin to see how your thoughts, emotions, actions and context are all connected and can be set off by some sort of trigger event. That is the goal of this exercise: to learn to notice the connections between your thoughts, feelings and behaviours. Once you have this skill mastered, you will next be able to begin to change unhelpful or distorted thoughts and beliefs and to pay more attention to environmental factors.

With this concept in mind, I suggest you stop reading at the end of this chapter and start monitoring your thinking over the next several days. If there is a time when you notice yourself feeling a strong unwanted or unhelpful emotion, try to identify the trigger, what you thought, what you felt, what you did and your vulnerability factors going in to the situation. Try to do this at least three times over the coming week using the form on the previous two pages to help you. This will help you learn the skill of being mindful about the way you think or interpret events in your life as they happen.

The more mindful you become of the way you are thinking, the more opportunity you have to examine your thoughts to see if what you are thinking is actually helpful or true. If you decide that it is not helpful, or that your thinking is somehow distorted or illogical, you can then decide if you would like to change the way that you think.

CHAPTER 8

CHANGING YOUR THOUGHT PATTERNS

Alexa

After many failed attempts, I got pregnant. We were so happy. I went in for the four month check-up only to find that the baby had no heartbeat. The Devil really came against me then. 'See, this is your punishment for the baby you killed. See, God has been mad at you all this time ...'

I felt horrible. For the first time I realized that I did not just abort a 'blob of cells'. It was a precious baby made by God's hands and would have grown into a child the same as the baby I had just lost. It had a right to live a life.

Realizing this, I had a choice to make. Would I let the 'father of lies' speak death to me again, or would I choose to believe what God said. I asked myself, 'Do I have hope that I will see both my babies in heaven again one day, or not? Am I forgiven or not? Did Jesus really die for my mistakes, or not? Was there nothing I could do to change his love for me, or not?'

I chose to believe God. I accepted responsibility for what I had done, sought wise council and support, and, after some time, began to forgive myself and receive God's forgiveness.

It was not long after this that we started trying and finally got pregnant again.

NEW THOUGHTS – TOWARDS A BETTER LIFE

Now that you have learned to take problematic thoughts captive, you can begin to replace them with new thoughts and beliefs that contribute to a better quality of life and are more consistent with your goals and values.

In some cases, changing the way we think can propel our efforts to making positive material changes in the way we live. Some problems can be confronted, some threats defused. Other times our problems, difficulties and adversities may be resistant to change or may even be unchangeable – for example, past events that are over and done with, or situations that we have no control over. But changing the way we think about them can make them much more manageable and help us get out from under their shadow in the present and the future.

However, changing long-held beliefs doesn't just happen by logically telling ourselves that the old lies or unhelpful thoughts aren't true. We can know something is a lie or irrational, but still feel as though it is true:

- We might know someone is trustworthy, but feel jealous anyway.
- We might know something is really no big deal, but feel angry anyway.
- We might know we have nothing to fear, but feel anxious anyway.

When this disconnect between what we know and what we feel happens, it is easy to get stuck – enslaved to how we feel instead of having the freedom to live our lives based on what we value and know to be true. But there is a way to get unstuck. Experiences distorted by lies over time got us into a mess, and new experiences over time based on truth will get us out.

Let's unpack this a bit, then begin to try it out.

We interpret our sensory experiences as they happen, based on what we have learned from past experiences; this is how we bring order to our life. We develop categories and classifications that speed up our ability to process what's happening and make sense of things in real time. This allows us to predict what will and won't work in the future. What is safe or dangerous, good or bad, possible or impossible before we take action.

But, at times, we misinterpret things. We thought something was dangerous, so we were fearful. But then we confronted our fear – maybe for some reason we were forced to do so or had a lot of support and encouragement to do so. And it turned out that the thing we were afraid of wasn't dangerous at all and there truly was nothing to be afraid of, or that the risk could be managed.

For example, as children, we may have been afraid of the dark, going to school for the first time or eating green beans. As we grew older, we learned that none of these things were dangerous and there was no reason to fear them.

Adults do the same. Driving a car in heavy traffic for the first time, public speaking, asking somebody for something you want like a date or a promotion – all these things that might seem dangerous and provoke anxiety are things most people are commonly forced to confront at some point in their life. When they do, it often turns out not to be as bad as they thought, or different from distressing situations experienced in the past that were intruding in unhelpful ways on the present. The individual gets a new experience of the situation in the present, disentangles themselves from the lies or unhelpful thoughts grounded in the past, and the negative emotions go away. As more robust thoughts and attitudes become embedded in your mental map, you will become more capable of weathering stressful situations in the future without compromising your values.

The key to making your feelings match your beliefs is to create new experiences that challenge or disturb unhelpful beliefs that have come from past experiences. When you do this again and again, over time your old ways of thinking and feeling will lose their grip on you, and your new way of thinking will begin to *feel* more and more true.

For example, Malik's conception of confession changed as he watched others he respected confess their mistakes and failures. This challenged his thinking about what it meant to be 'sober' from his behavioural addictions, and vastly improved his relapse recovery time:

Malik

The spiritual discipline of confession to others and to God that we practice in step five was life-changing for me. I witnessed men with years of sobriety sit in Open Share with their heads hung low from acting out. I saw leaders break their sobriety and confess. I learned that nothing should be hidden and that we are called to be open and honest.

I used to believe that sobriety meant perfection. If I slipped, I was done; it was a downhill pathway to a new lower bottom with another painful return after spending years in addictive, destructive behaviour. I now realize that sobriety is not a pathway of perfection; what is important is how fast you can get back on your feet. How quickly you can admit that you were wrong, step out of denial, and pick up where you left off without having to find a new lower bottom. I realized with that model that I can become consistent, trustworthy and reliable. My sobriety is not the biggest thing; my faith in God is the most important thing. The sobriety will follow when the focus on behaviour is rooted in my relationship with God.

It was Malik's firm belief that he had value in God's sight, and was made for a purpose, that gave him the courage to confess – whatever the result might be. His beliefs about himself had changed. He was no longer basing his value on how well he performed, or how much he had, and hiding his flaws. Now, believing that he was safe in Christ, he could talk openly about what he had kept hidden in the past for fear of rejection. His worldview finally connected him to his roots, and his roots to the living water that sustained him when he made mistakes and felt convicted about confessing them in order to get help for something he could not handle on his own.

Laura is another example. She was challenged by a counsellor to rethink the way she perceived her struggles with alcohol, which she initially resisted.

Laura

I remember this counsellor telling me that I needed to develop a spirit of desperation about recovery and quickly, to my surprise, I became very desperate to recover. He also told me that one day I would consider my addiction a gift. At the time he spoke those words to me, I wanted to kill him … or at least scratch his eyes out.

A few months into this journey, our pastor at church preached a sermon about helping others, and a few months later I was asking how I could help other women and use the difficulties in my life – my gift – in the lives of others. As I've trusted God to use my struggles, I have grown significantly in the Lord.

I now realize that addiction was for me just a symptom of deeper areas the Lord wanted to touch and heal. I do not regret the past or wish to shut the door on it or have it painted over. Struggling with alcohol is to some a despicable, misunderstood lack of control. I've learned that my struggle is exactly the vehicle that God used to show me my desperate need of him. I will never regret that nor keep that to myself. This truth has caused me to become transparent in my relationships.

If God can use my struggles to help another person, who am I to stand in the way of his work?

SIX STEPS TO CREATING NEW THOUGHTS AND EXPERIENCES

Although the thoughts of Malik and Laura were challenged and changed through their organic interactions with other people, there is a way to stimulate this process so that you can become intentional about challenging unhelpful thoughts and beliefs in your life.

Below are six steps that can help you create new thoughts and actions to go with them. By acting on your new thoughts, like Laura and Malik did, you will begin to have new experiences that help your new way of thinking begin to feel true to you.

I will first give you an overview of these steps, so you know something about this new skill you are about to practice. In the next section, you will identify a thought or belief that is either unhelpful or untrue and use the Functional Thoughts and Actions Plan (FTAP) to work through each step.

For now, don't worry about processing an actual thought. Just read through the steps to get an idea of what the process will look like.

1. Capture the thought that is fuelling negative emotions and behaviours. You learned to do that using the Distressing Thought Form.
2. Begin to question or test the problematic thought by asking yourself a series of questions about it, which are included in the Functional Thoughts and Actions Plan (FTAP) just ahead.

In some ways, this process is like thinking about the problematic thought as a 3D object that you have pulled out of the darkness and are holding up to the light in order to look at it from different perspectives. Examining it in a thoughtful way, rather than simply accepting it without thinking.

It is important to note that not every question listed on the FTAP will apply to every thought that you want to examine. If a question seems fit to purpose, use it. If not, feel free to leave it and move on to the next question.

3. After testing the thought, you may find it was not true, not helpful or not effective at helping you to live in a way that reflects your values, beliefs and goals in life. If that is the case, then you will use the information you generated in step two to create a new thought that will replace the old thought. It may help to base your new thought on a particular verse or section of Scripture. If Scripture does not address the specific situation that you are facing, it might be helpful to connect your new thought to biblical themes or aspects of God's character such as love, justice, mercy, etc.

4. This is where the rubber meets the road. It is now time to create what you might wish to think of as a behavioural experiment where you actually begin to *act* based on your new way of thinking. They are called experiments because you are only just beginning to try out a new way of living to see what happens. This is similar to the 'acting as if', 'fake it 'til you make it' or 'walk by faith not by sight' approaches commonly taken in recovery and discipleship.

5. Unfortunately, there is no guarantee that things will work exactly the way you hope. That is why the fifth step is very important, which is to create a fall-back plan, or plan B, just in case plan A doesn't work out. If things go wrong in your experiment, what will you do? How will you continue to act based on what you have decided to be true or helpful in step three?

For example, you might choose to believe that because you have inherent worth, and have been a hard worker, it is completely appropriate for you to ask for a promotion. And it may well be! So you ask your boss for one, and get denied without just cause. That doesn't mean you don't deserve that promotion.

Perhaps you not getting the promotion has nothing to do with you. Maybe your company just doesn't have the money, or the executives are greedy and unjust. What will you do if the worst happens and you are denied? How will you cope well, continuing to believe that you are worthy of more responsibility and a pay rise? Perhaps you decide that if you are denied the promotion, you will keep working and building your CV whilst looking for a job elsewhere, or even develop your own business in your spare time.

This approach is meant to help you to see that you have options – you are not completely at the mercy of events outside your influence. You have the ability to live out your beliefs, even in the face of adversity or difficulty, and are not powerless against such things.

6. Next you can document what happened and what you learned when you conducted your behavioural experiment. This will help you to remember what you did and how you did it. It also gives you a space to record the amazing ways in which God is at work in your life as you begin to act on your faith in more and more areas.

PERSEVERE

Remember, one new experience of success may not be enough to help you feel as though your new thought is true. You may have to act in a way that is congruent with your beliefs over and over again before they begin to feel as true in your heart as they are in your head. But if you keep it up, over time the truth will slowly begin to sink in.

The FTAP will walk you through each of the six steps described above. As you use this method to confront problematic thoughts again and again, you will get more and more familiar with the form. Soon, you will begin to remember how the FTAP works, and will be able to confront problematic thoughts using this method without needing to look at the FTAP itself.

FUNCTIONAL THOUGHTS AND ACTIONS PLAN

Step one: Identify the Thought to be Tested

What is the thought, attitude, belief or opinion that is either not true, or is causing problems in my life?

What emotions go with this thought, attitude, belief or opinion?

What behaviours do I do, or did I do, when thinking this way?

Step two: Question the Thought

How will this thought or belief help me attain my goals in life?

How will this thought or belief help me to have healthy relationships?

How will this thought or belief help me to live out my faith or values?

What is the evidence that this thought or belief is true?

What is the evidence that this thought or belief is not true?

Is there another explanation or interpretation?

What is the worst that can happen in the problematic situation?

How can I cope well with that?

What is the best that can happen in the problematic situation?

What is the most likely thing that will happen?

If I had a friend in a similar situation, what would I tell them?

What is the overall effect of continuing to believe or repeat this thought or belief?

What would be the effect of me changing this thought or belief?

Should I change my way of thinking?

Step Three: New Thought

Based on the above, what is a new way of thinking or believing that more effectively helps me deal with this situation and/or be the person I want to be?

How do I feel now, thinking this new thought?

Is there Scripture that goes with this new way of thinking?

Step four: Experiment

What can I plan to do that will go with my new way of thinking? (Try to make a plan that you control, that is observable, simple, measurable, intentional and something you can do consistently. Gauge your success based on what you can do, not on other people's responses or outcomes over which you have no control.)

Step five: Backup Plan

If that doesn't work out, what is my backup plan?

Step Six: Document What Happened

What have I learned? What happened in my experiment?

CHAPTER 9

WORKING WITH UNHELPFUL EMOTIONS

Smile, though your heart is aching
Smile, even though it's breaking.
When there are clouds in the sky
you'll get by.

If you smile through your fear and sorrow
Smile and maybe tomorrow
You'll see the sun come shining through
For you.

'SMILE'[17]

EMOTIONS ARE WONDERFUL

Emotions add colour and vibrancy to life. They can also prompt us to take fast action when there isn't time to think, giving us 'gut feelings' that guide us through uncertainty, or providing extra fuel to tackle tough situations.

We are made in God's image, and God himself is described in Scripture as having emotions. He is said at different times to be:

---

17 Composed by Charlie Chaplin 1936; lyrics by John Turner and Geoffrey Parsons, 1954.

Grieved

*How often they rebelled against him in the wilderness
and grieved him in the wasteland!*

PSALM 78:40 NIV

Angry

*As for me, the LORD was also angry with me on your
account. He said, 'You also will not be able to go there.'*

DEUTERONOMY 1:37

Pleased

The LORD was pleased that Solomon made this request.

1 KINGS 3:10

Joyful and Loving

*The LORD your God is in your midst;
he is a warrior who can deliver.
He takes great delight in you;
he renews you by his love;
he shouts for joy over you.*

ZEPHANIAH 3:17

Moved by Pity

*When the LORD raised up leaders for them, the LORD
was with each leader and delivered the people from their
enemies while the leader remained alive. The LORD felt sorry
for them when they cried out in agony because of what their
harsh oppressors did to them.*

JUDGES 2:18

However, we would be wise not to make the mistake of thinking that God's 'emotions' are just like ours. God, the Father, is spirit (John 4:24), not human. He is also impassible. That means he is constant and unfailing. He is not, in a fit of anger, going to sin or do something to harm us that he later regrets – something humans do in their anger routinely. In the same way, God's love for us is not fickle like human love. It is steadfast, loyal, consistent, decisive and unchanging. He never falls out of love with us.

Why then is God often described as launching into action in the heat of emotion? Fortunately, there is a simple answer for this question:

The Bible is literature inspired by the Holy Spirit who wrote through human authors, and it uses different literary devices to communicate complex truths about a limitless God in ways that we limited humans (by comparison) can understand. For example, when Scripture says that God walked with Adam 'in the garden in the cool of the day,' (Genesis 3:8 NIV) it is not meant to imply that God has feet and walks in the same way that we do. God is spirit, and as such, does not have feet. That is an anthropomorphism, which means that human terminology has been ascribed to something that is not human (God in spirit form).

In some way, God's presence was with Adam in the garden, and the author of Genesis (traditionally thought to be Moses) wrote that God walked with Adam to communicate that they spent time with one another in an intimate way. Therefore, whenever you are reading the Old Testament and see God described as doing something with a hand, or eyes or hair etc., it is important to recognize that this is metaphorical description meant to convey something mystical and supernatural that God is doing, using terms that humans can understand.

A similar literary device is used when it comes to ascribing emotions to God. For example, there are times when God, in his anger, appears to contemplate doing certain things, and then changes his mind. These are what are called anthropopathisms – the emotional equivalent of anthropomorphisms.

When Scripture communicates that God is overwhelmed with emotion, that is a way to communicate that he is not unaffected by what we do. He is not cold and distant. He is intimately involved with us. Yet his 'emotion' is of a higher quality. He is able to communicate anger, yet still remain totally connected in a love relationship and acts in a way that, from an eternal perspective, is perfectly consistent with his character and goals.

This is hard for us to understand and has led to some people proposing solutions that diminish the unchanging nature or sovereignty of God (such as open theism) to explain his emotions. However, it is possible that what we experience as God's anger may be more akin to 'basking in the light of the moon'. The moon, of course, is a rock that merely reflects light from the sun. Yet, from our vantage point it appears to be shining down on us. Perhaps what the Old Testament writers experienced as God's anger from their vantage point is in some way not what it appears to be.

Jesus, on the other hand, was human and by limiting his own deity, did experience human emotions. He felt:

Compassion

When he saw the crowds, he had compassion on them because they were bewildered and helpless, like sheep without a shepherd.

MATTHEW 9:36

Love

My commandment is this – to love one another just as I have loved you.

JOHN 15:12

Distress

When Jesus saw her weeping, and the people who had come with her weeping, he was intensely moved in spirit and greatly distressed.

JOHN 11:33

Sadness

Jesus wept.

JOHN 11:35

Anger and grief

After looking around at them in anger, grieved by the hardness of their hearts, he said to the man, 'Stretch out your hand.' He stretched it out, and his hand was restored.

MARK 3:5

Temptation

For we do not have a high priest incapable of sympathizing with our weaknesses, but one who has been tempted in every way just as we are, yet without sin.

HEBREWS 4:15

Once again, while Jesus was fully human (and fully God) he experienced human emotion, and yet it did not cause him to violate his own nature. He drew from his emotional human side, yet retained his sense of value, purpose, mission and identity. He did the same when experiencing intense emotional and physical pain during his betrayal, torture and execution.

Part of becoming more and more like Christ is about learning how to handle our conflicting emotions in a way that still allows us to reach our goals and live out our values. Christlikeness involves the recognition that our emotions are a good thing – that they are in fact part of the image of God we are made in (in some mysterious way), but they are not to rule us. At times, we will have conflicting emotions about someone or something – in the same way that Jesus could love, and also be angry with, someone at the same time.

For example, we may like and dislike, or even love and hate, someone at the same time. The people in our lives are not always all good *or* all bad. Sometimes they are a mixture of both at different places and times. People and relationships are a complex mix of attributes, and they change from season to season – sometimes they can change rapidly in even a single day, hour, or minute!

Another principle is that it is possible to act against how you feel: for example, to be angry, but still act in a loving way towards those you are committed to loving; to be fearful, but still act in a brave way when your values demand courage in the face of adversity; to be sad but still smile, in hope that eventually the sad feelings will pass. Perhaps the smile on your face will entangle itself in the world around you, eliciting a positive response from others which then comes back to you in a way that broadens your smile.

This is known as the 'fake it 'til you make it' strategy, which is very useful when someone is in the beginning stages of abstinence and the good feelings associated with their addictive activity of choice are no longer available. They have to lean into life at this stage, doing what they know is good for them, but that does not yet feel good. This is because their body has forgotten how to produce natural feel-good chemicals like serotonin in response to natural events such as sleeping, eating or healthy relationships.

It is also an act of walking by faith, not by sight (2 Corinthians 5:7). It is about living according to your values, and value-based goals, not transient emotions. Hence some Christians use the term '*faith* it 'til you make it'. We're not faking it at all; we're acting on what we know to be true by faith. Learning to do this can help us become more like God, who may have had conflicting 'emotions' at times, but never lets these feelings cause him to do something that would be inconsistent with his character, goals or values.

Being made in God's image, we all have the capacity to move towards the same level of maturity. If you are a Christ-follower, then the Holy Spirit is at work in you to help you along the path towards maturity in this area of your life. You also have another wonderful advantage: Scripture gives you an unchanging standard of truth to live by, so that when it may be difficult to sort out your feelings, you can always look to God's word for guidance.

It is, however, important to remember that we will always struggle to handle our conflicting emotions perfectly. This is why we are so dependent on and grateful for God's endless grace.

These are all good things for us to keep in mind as we seek to become more like Christ in our emotional lives. To that end, we are going to focus on skills that help us govern our unhelpful or unwanted emotions.

GOVERNING OUR EMOTIONS

Emotions can be painful, problematic, extremely pleasant and everything in between. Sometimes we have the space to allow ourselves to explore our emotions or feel them deeply. At other times, we may need to put our emotions aside so that we can function, concentrate on something important or maintain our integrity.

Nevertheless, there is a time for all emotions, even in the extreme. For example, it is appropriate to be angry about injustice (Psalm 7:11), to grieve when someone has died (1 Thessalonians 4:13), and to love deeply and with delight (Song of Songs 1:2) within the biblical parameters for appropriate love relationships.

Yet emotions can also be based on our entanglements with false assumptions, unsubstantiated beliefs, distorted thinking or untruths. And even when there is good evidence to believe that something is true, and when strong emotion is justified, it can still be destructive or at least counter-productive to long-term goals and values when acted upon.

For example: just because you really want something that isn't yours, is not a legal defence for stealing. Nor would many people in a committed relationship or marriage accept strong feelings for another person as justification for infidelity.

Thankfully, there is an alternative to just 'going with' an emotion. We can instead choose to 'act against' the emotion to prevent violating our values or damaging our ability to attain long-term goals.

HOW TO ACT AGAINST UNWANTED OR UNHELPFUL EMOTIONS

In our last chapter we learned a way to think (and then act) our way out of unhelpful or unwanted behaviours and emotions. This strategy helps you act your way out of the unwanted or unhelpful feelings, which can in turn lead to more healthy thought patterns as well.

Acting against an unwanted or unhelpful emotion means doing the right thing, the helpful thing, the effective thing, even when you don't feel like it or when it's hard or uncomfortable. Deanna had that experience when she first reached out to her church for help after it became clear that managing life on her terms simply wasn't working.

Deanna

In February, I remember feeling particularly low. For months, I had not been able to hear from God through Scripture and my prayers felt hollow. My quiet times felt useless. I felt useless. I was wishing for a car accident or cancer diagnosis to take me from this world. At one point

I held up my hands to God and said, 'Lord, my faith has dwindled to the size of a mustard seed, no more. I can't pray or read or move forward in faith. Please help me.' I was at the end of myself and my thinking.

That same month, there was an advert in the church bulletin: 'Are you struggling with hurts, habits or hang-ups in your life? Is there a relationship in your life that isn't working?' Well, I was living with hurt every day and my daughter and I practically hated each other. So when my church launched a group that could help me with those issues in March, I chose to attend. It required humility to walk through the doors of a recovery group meeting, but my methods of handling life were not working and I needed help.

First, name your emotion. A growing body of research supports the idea that naming emotions releases chemicals in the brain that help us calm down.[18] Naming emotions engages the part of the brain responsible for logic and reason and may give you some distance from the emotion. If you still feel compelled to do whatever it is that the emotion is compelling you to do, then:

Play it out. Imagine yourself doing what you feel like doing, and then imagine what the long-term results or consequences might be. Ask yourself, 'Will doing what I feel like doing right now help me live out my values or achieve my long-term goals?'

If the answer is YES, then feel free to give in to the urge to do what you feel like doing. However, if you act on your emotions, be ready and willing to accept the consequences of your actions. If it doesn't work out the way you hoped it would, allow that experience to instruct you. Use what you learn to try a different approach next time if that is what is called for to live out your faith and values.

If the answer is NO, then don't act on your emotion. Instead, act against your feelings.

18 Jared B. Torre, Matthew Lieberman, 'Putting Feelings Into Words: Affect labeling as Implicit Emotion Regulation' *Emotion Review* 10, vol 1, 2, (2018), pp. 116-124.

To refer back to Deanna's example, her emotions of anger, hopelessness and depression may have led her to lash out in her relationships, isolate herself from God and others, or even do something to harm herself. Instead, when an offer for help appeared, she swallowed her pride and reached out for help.

The list of emotions below contains several possible suggestions as to how you might choose to act against a particular emotion. Take a moment to review each emotion in the list. Ask yourself if there is a particular emotion that prompts you to take actions, or harbour attitudes, that are destructive or unhelpful. If you aren't sure, ask God if there's anything he is calling you to address. You might also ask someone you trust, who knows you well, if there is a particular emotion that seems to lead you away from your goals and values when it pops up.

Anger

Prompts us to attack or defend ourselves, others, our goals, our values. There are times this may be appropriate. However, if acting on our anger becomes counter-productive, we can choose to act against it:

- Be nice instead.
- Gently disengage yourself from the situation.
- Use a gentle tone of voice rather than a harsh tone.
- Avoid the person you feel like attacking, but in a kind way.
- Use humour or play to lighten the situation.
- Try forgiving or seeing the situation from the other person's perspective.
- Be aware of your body language. Smile a little. Relax your muscles.
- Other _____.

Deanna

My impatience and sharpness in telling the girls to get ready for bed was evident. My second daughter, then eleven, ignored me and continued her activity. When she ignored me, I raised my voice and commanded her to bed. She gave me a haughty look and walked slowly to her room. I could feel the anger rising in me. Well, shouldn't a disobedient child be corrected?! So I followed her and let her know that she was being rude and should apologize (never mind that I was being rude and disrespectful myself). She knew the dynamic and dutifully apologized, but she didn't mean it. My anger turned to rage, and I made it clear she was not treating me with respect. I finally got the reaction of tears, which must have meant that she got the lesson. I left the room, but strangely felt convicted that my anger was not right. I went back and apologized. She wouldn't accept it. I went back to my room and cried in pain once again, convicted that I was a failure at parenting.

I heard a whisper in my mind telling me to go and tell her that I loved her. My next thought was 'no,' I would see her in the morning. I tried to distract myself with TV, but again felt the strong message that I should go to my daughter and tell her that I love her. When I went into her room, I saw that her bed was empty. The light was on in the bathroom and I could hear water running. Panic surged in my heart. I got her to open the door and saw her face was red and swollen from crying. She was hiding her hands behind her back. I asked what she was holding, and she shrugged. I asked again, and she showed me. She had been trying to cut her wrists with scissors. She was eleven years old. I cried and held her. We cried together for what seemed like hours. I didn't mention that my sister cut her arms in high school due to pain from abuse. Here was that tragedy in my own home. This time I was the disconnected mum.

Sadness

Prompts us to avoid, shut down, withdraw, give up, become negative, irritable and have a hard time remembering anything good from the past. There are times when it may make sense and can even be healthy to be sad – grieving is one of them. However, if acting on our sadness becomes counter-productive, or we need to take a break from working through our grief (so that we can function in life when certain times or situations demand it, or just to recharge our batteries enough to continue the grieving process), we can choose to act against it:

- Try to smile – even just a little.
- Get out and do something – see what happens.
- Connect with other people.
- Do things that make us laugh.
- Serve someone else.
- Get perspective through stories of other people who have faced similar challenges.
- Remember the good times.
- Other _____.

Fear

Prompts us to run, hide, beg, freeze, babble, cry, sweat or tremble. There are times when it may make sense to be afraid. However, we might find that while it makes sense to be afraid, it is not helping us to confront the situation that we are afraid of. When acting on our fear is counter-productive to our goals or values, we can act against it:

- Act brave.
- Maintain boundaries and limits.
- Approach and engage with what we are afraid of, over and over, until we are no longer afraid.
- Get help.

- Move to a square, confident posture. Make eye contact.
- Other _____.

Disgust

Prompts us to avoid, gag, get away, distance ourselves, not look, speak in a condescending way, feel unclean or sick to our stomach. It may make sense to feel disgusted by something, but then again there may be times when acting on our disgust will be counter-productive to our goals and values. When that happens, we can act against it:

- Approach when we feel like avoiding.
- Research what we feel like avoiding; get educated about it.
- If appropriate, do what we are disgusted by, again and again, until it is tolerable.
- Try being kind to the people we are disgusted by.
- Other _____.

Love/Attraction

Prompts us to express affection, physical and otherwise. It may make sense to love someone that is attractive to us (physically, or because of shared values and admirable qualities). However, if acting on our love is counter-productive to our values and beliefs, or long-term goals, we can act against it:

- Get away, avoid.
- Avoid things and places that remind us of the person.
- Remember our values and goals.
- Remember the long-term effect of acting on our love.
- Stop giving signals that you're interested.
- Engage with different people, places or things.
- Other _____.

The above five emotions are fairly straightforward. The next two are a bit more complex as the method of 'acting against' the emotion involves discerning whether the emotion makes sense given our values, and how to skilfully respond in the case that it does or doesn't. Read through them carefully.

Guilt

- Guilt is the feeling that lets us know that what we did violates our moral principles.
- If we have violated our moral principles, then guilt makes sense. A response-able reaction to guilt in many situations is to pray about whether or not it is appropriate to offer the offended party an amends. A complete amends entails the following five steps:
  - Admit it.
  - Apologize for what was done.
  - Empathize with how the other person felt.
  - Repay or repair whatever was lost, broken, missed, etc.
  - Commit to a plan of change so you don't repeat the offence.
- However, at the same time we need to bear in mind the following:
  - Realize that making complete amends does not mean we will be immediately forgiven or reconciled. That is up to the person we've hurt.
  - Rest knowing that we've done everything we can do.
  - Keep working our change-plan to rebuild trust.
  - (see Chapter 12 for more detailed information on making amends).
- If we have not violated our own moral principles, and we have nothing to feel guilty about (for example, feeling guilty about leaving an abusive relationship):
  - Examine our thoughts to find out where the guilty feeling comes from.

- Do what we feel guilty about again and again until you are comfortable.
- Find a community that can help support you as you seek to grow and change.
- Other _____.

Shame

Shame is a complex emotion, and there is a large literature around it. Below are a few key points to consider when trying to decide if what we are feeling is shame, and what to do about it:

- Shame is something usually felt in relationship to others. It is an emotional response to the exposure, or potential exposure, of an action that others will think of as being bad or wrong. Feelings of shame may be incited in us when others:
  - treat us as though we are worthless, bad or unlovable
  - accuse us of wrongdoing
  - reject us
  - ridicule us.

- In its most damaging form, shame communicates that not only is the offence wrong or bad, but that the person who committed the offence is as bad, unacceptable and irredeemable as their actions. This is the diabolical inversion of the biblical standard (explained at length in Chapter 1) which is that every human being is made in God's image and as such has an unconditional, inherent value.

- People who are abused as children have no defence against the accusation that they are bad, unlovable or worthless – they have not yet developed the inner strength and positive sense of self needed to reject these claims. This is especially true when they are shamed (told they are bad or defective) by parents who are supposed to love them. It is often less painful for children to accept that they are bad and therefore deserving of the abuse, than it is for them to believe their parents do not love them (because the parents themselves are hurt people, and as such are not capable of providing healthy love).

- Abused children who absorb shame messages may learn to cope with their pain in ways that are destructive and culturally unacceptable (drugs, alcohol, unhealthy sexual patterns, self-harm etc.) or destructive but culturally rewarded (workaholism, perfectionism, self-sacrificing). Either can lead to negative consequences, which then reinforce shameful feelings. This horrible shame cycle can go on for decades before the person recognizes the source of their compulsions lies in their abuse or neglect as children, which was not (is *never*) their fault. If you were abused as a child and have never talked to someone about it, I strongly urge you to seek further support from a trusted mentor or counsellor. One thing they can help you to do is identify shame messages you may have internalized, and the ways in which those messages have affected your choices in the past and present.

- Shame messages can be rejected. There are biblical examples of people who knew they had no reason to feel shame because they were innocent (Genesis 2:25, 1 John 2:28), and Jesus rejected the shame of the cross despite the fact that crucifixion was designed to be a humiliating experience in which the victim was stripped of clothing, beaten and openly mocked (Hebrews 12:2).

- Though this clashes with mainstream conceptualizations of shame as being always toxic, there are biblical examples of shame being used in a non-abusive, corrective fashion, signalling to the offending party that their actions had been noticed, were affecting the group and were deemed to be unacceptable (2 Thessalonians 3:14). The point of this was restoration within the group. The way that restoration was affected was by withdrawing from the person and not enabling the behaviour (in this case in Thessalonica, the withdrawal meant no longer providing food for someone who was capable of work but not willing to work). This same strategy is often employed by people in relationship with someone who is abusing substances, endangering themselves and taking advantage of others to support their habit. By withdrawing all support and making a demand as a group that the person struggling with addiction enter treatment, the clear message is sent that this behaviour will no longer be tolerated or enabled.

In Summary, a good way to deal with shame is:

- If the thing that we feel ashamed about is a violation of our own moral principles:
  - Realize that your behaviour does not define your value.
  - Examine your thoughts regarding your value.
  - Examine the source of your shameful feelings.
  - Follow steps for dealing with guilt when you have broken your own moral principles, i.e., make amends.
  - Seek restoration within the group.
- If the thing that we feel ashamed of is not a violation of our own moral principles:
  - Realize that your behaviour does not define your value.
  - Examine your thoughts regarding your value.
  - Examine the source of your shameful feelings.
  - Consider joining a group that won't shame you *or* seek to influence your current group from within to change its values (if possible).
  - Follow steps for dealing with guilt when you've *not* broken your own moral principles.

Lauren

*By the end, I was absolutely sick with fear. It truly was insanity,
like two sides of a coin: on one side was absolute terror that I
would be found out, and on the other that old lie that no one
really knew me or loved me … if they did, they would know
that I was destroying myself. Finally, the pain of my condition
exceeded my fear of being exposed. I lay in bed one night with
my husband and couldn't stop crying. I told him everything.
He could not have loved me more perfectly in that moment.
He lived out the 'for better or worse, in sickness and in health'
part of our vows that night, and I am so grateful! I felt such
incredible shame and cried out to the Lord for mercy. He
met me so personally right there in that shame, and at that
moment, I realized the shame that Jesus wore on the cross
2,000 years ago was mine. He understood exactly what I was
experiencing. In that hard place I received his mercy, and
intimacy with him began again, sinner to Saviour. Broken
little lost lamb to Shepherd.*

WRITE AND REFLECT

Which emotion tends to cause the most difficulties in
your life? How?

What strategies will you experiment with to try to 'act against' the emotions?

Experiment with your plan to act against the emotion that causes difficulty in your life. Record the results in your journal. Many people find that, in low-level emotion situations, the 'act against' strategy works best. For situations where emotions are more intense or even overwhelming, the strategies in the next section may be more helpful.

OVERWHELMING STRESS

Sometimes we are in distress because we can't do anything to change the situation, and we haven't been fully able to change our thoughts about it either. Even when we act against it, it seems impossible to change the way we feel.

In such times, we need relief from our distress so that we are not overwhelmed to the point of giving up or giving in. Research indicates that when a person is overly stressed, the part of their brain responsible for logic and reason begins to shut down and the part responsible for emotion takes over.[19] That's why it is so hard to think logically when emotions run high.

Once we are relieved from distress, we can begin to think more rationally again and use our other skills to deal effectively

19 Bita Moghaddam, 'The Complicated Relationship of Stress and Prefrontal Cortex'. *Biological Psychiatry* 80, vol 10, (2016): 728-729.

with the situation. In such times, the most effective thing we can do for ourselves is not to engage in the problem or situation that is triggering the emotional response. If we do, we may wind up acting out in a way that threatens our goals or violates our values.

It may be that the thing we are feeling emotional about is perfectly justified and does need to be confronted at some point. However, when we are completely overwhelmed with emotion, we need to find a way to come back to an emotional baseline before we can confront the situation effectively. Once we do, the part of our brain responsible for logical reasoning and goal-directed behaviour *will* come back online again and help us make a more effective plan to deal with the distressing situation.

If we are prone to becoming overwhelmed with emotion, it is important that we learn to accept this about ourselves. There is no shame in it. Quite the opposite. It takes tremendous self-insight to know and understand our triggers, and a strong commitment to our principles to manage emotions effectively when it would be much easier to just do or say whatever we feel, come what may.

Also, if you tend to be an emotionally responsive person, it is important to see this as a gift from God that can be used for great good! It could be that our emotionality helps us to pick up on things that others would be insensitive to. We may have a stronger sense of intuition or empathy, and it is important to learn to trust and use these gifts. However, we will be able to make even better use of them when we can communicate our intuition clearly and rationally so that others can more easily hear and understand our insights.

You are the expert on yourself, so you know best the times in your life when you feel most overwhelmed. Sometimes this is predictable – there are certain situations in our lives that reoccur and trigger us every time. These are easier to deal with because of their regularity. We know what happens and how we tend to respond. Other overwhelming situations may be impossible to predict and are a bit more challenging to prepare for ahead of time.

Whatever the case, if we think it is possible that we will face a situation that could lead to us feeling overwhelmed with emotion, we can plan ahead for what we will do when it happens so that we don't have to think of what to do, we can just follow our plan.

Make your plan when you are calm, centred and able to draw on your resources. You may also wish to create a way to remind yourself of the plan when you are overwhelmed so that you don't have to try to recall it when you are under stress.

WHEN YOU CAN'T THINK STRAIGHT

The following is a list of things we can do when we are so overwhelmed with emotion that we aren't able to think straight. This is not about going into denial. You know the situation is there and needs to be dealt with. You just need a break so that you are able to think clearly and get some perspective. You can decide which options on this list will work best for you, add to this list or create your own list.

Re-centring Options
- Leave the situation.
- Get some work done.
- Do something fun and active.
- Watch a movie.
- Read a book.
- Listen to music.
- Play an instrument.
- Cook.
- Eat something delicious.
- Take a hot bath or a cold shower.
- Smell something nice – aromatherapy.
- Snuggle a pet.

- Get outside.
- Look at something beautiful.
- Do intense physical exercise.
- Journal to express thoughts and feelings.
- Talk to someone you trust.
- Listen to a podcast.
- Pray earnestly.
- Read the Bible.
- Serve someone who is struggling – get outside yourself.
- Knit.

A few key things to remember when you're doing a re-centring activity:

Activities with lots of little, achievable short-term goals are best. When we do these types of activities, we tend to forget about the rest of the world and become totally focused. The activity demands our full attention.

- Remember to 'take one moment at a time'.
- Remember that you have never had an emotion that lasted forever. It is normal to have bad feelings from time to time. It will pass – especially as you begin doing your distraction activity.
- Remember to reflect on your long-term goals, beliefs and higher values.

Once you are calm and centred again, you can use your other LifeCare skills to address the situation in a more productive way.

WRITE AND REFLECT

What situations do you face that have the potential to cause overwhelming stress?

What strategies will you experiment with to help you get some distance from the situation and return to an emotional baseline?

Experiment with different techniques that can help you calm down and begin to think clearly. Notice what works and what doesn't. When you find something that works, plan ahead to make it as simple as possible to use this strategy when you need it most. You might even plan to schedule these types of activities into your day or week, so that you always have time and space to reflect and re-centre.

PROBLEM-SOLVING

Sometimes, when emotions run high it's not because of unclear thinking. Nor is our feeling out of line with our values. Instead, it is because there is a legitimate problem that needs to be solved, or some difficulty that needs to be overcome.

For example, rent might be due when we don't have the money. Our boss might give us a task that we don't know how to complete. We might feel that we are in danger but be unsure about how to get to safety. A friend or relative might be in trouble and we don't feel like we know how to help.

In this case, the emotion we are experiencing may well be appropriate for our situation. That is, we may have legitimate, rational reasons for feeling afraid, hurt, sad or angry and our emotions may be telling us that it is important for us to pay attention to this situation.

When that happens, while calming ourselves down will help us think more clearly, ultimately it is solving the problem that will help resolve the situation. Our emotions will settle down in turn. The following is a simple Problem-Solving Strategy that can help us think through how we might begin to resolve a problem in our lives:

1. Define the problem. Try to be as objective as possible.
2. Make sure you have all the facts. Don't leave anything out.
3. Looking at all the facts, redefine the problem if necessary. What needs to be solved?
4. Generate a list of potential solutions.
5. Pick the best solution.
6. Develop a Pro/Con list:
    a. If the cons outweigh the pros, return to Step 5.
    b. If the pros outweigh the cons, go to Step 7.
7. Implement the solution.

8. Evaluate the outcome:
    a. If it works, keep doing it.
    b. If it needs tweaking, tweak it.
    c. If it isn't working at all, return to Step 5.

WRITE AND REFLECT

Pick a legitimate problem in your life – something that you are not sure what to do about. Maybe something that you are experiencing some distress over. Use the Problem-Solving Strategy above to try and come up with a solution, filling in each step using the form.

Problem Solving Strategy

1. Define the problem. Try to be as objective as possible.

2. Make sure you have all the facts. Don't leave anything out.

3. Looking at all the facts, redefine the problem if necessary. What needs to be solved?

4. Generate a list of potential solutions.

5. Pick the best solution.

6. Develop a Pro/Con list:
    a. If the cons outweigh the pros, return to Step 5.
    b. If the pros outweigh the cons, go to Step 7.

Solution	Pro	Con
	1.	1.
	2.	2.
	3.	3.
	4.	4.

7. Implement the solution. How did it work?

8. Evaluate the outcome:
   a. If it works, keep doing it.
   b. If it needs tweaking, tweak it.
   c. If it isn't working at all, return to Step 5.

This basic Problem-Solving Strategy can be helpful in defining your problem, thinking through your options and resources and generating solutions.

However, sometimes it is not our own rationality, emotions or skill-based problems that we need to solve. Sometimes, problems involve other people who are not cooperating with our best efforts to address the situation. We may know people like this. No matter what we say or do, the message we attempt to communicate just doesn't seem to be received in the way we intended. And when we practice acting on our inherent value in Christ by asserting ourselves and asking for what we want, instead of understanding and acceptance, we are met with hostility and rejection.

Does this mean we are not valuable or acceptable? Does it mean we are not thinking rationally, or that we have done something wrong?

Not necessarily. It may be that, in this situation, with this particular person, what we need are some additional communication skills. Perhaps God is allowing us to go through this difficult time in order to help us learn how to ask for what we want, and how to connect with someone who is emotionally distressed. If that is what you are experiencing, the next chapter will be useful to you.

CHAPTER 10

INTERPERSONAL SKILLS

Like apples of gold in settings of silver,
so is a word skillfully spoken.

PROVERBS 25:11

Through patience a ruler can be persuaded,
and a soft tongue can break a bone.

PROVERBS 25:15

Like a city that is broken down and without a wall,
so is a person who cannot control his temper.

PROVERBS 25:28

IT STARTS WITH LISTENING

It would be wonderful if we could just say what we mean, and everyone would always receive it in the spirit with which it was intended. However, we all know that there are times when the message intended is not the message received. Arguments or relational rifts can develop quickly based on simple miscommunication.

When this happens, people have less access to the part of their brain that is responsible for logical thinking. When both people in the argument think they are right, they tend to want to make the other person see their point of view, so each side makes their case more and more vigorously as tempers flare, and each side loses the ability to think rationally. This is known as escalation, and it is a recipe for disaster.

There is a better way, and it can easily be remembered by its acronym LEG:

- **Listen**

  Instead of defending your point of view, listen for what the other person wants that you can agree with. There will often be some underlying, basic, God-given human need that they are trying to meet – even if they are going about it in a way with which you disagree or that is contrary to Scripture.

- **Endorse**

  Endorse the part of the issue that makes sense to you. Once you identify the underlying God-given need, affirm it. Let them know that it makes sense that they would, for example, want to feel loved, understood, respected or accepted.

- **Goal**

  Tell the person what you will do in the future to help support them regarding the need or issue that is important to you both. Don't agree to do things that violate your faith, values or boundaries. Look for common ground or opportunities to at least meet halfway.

The best time to employ this strategy is at the first sign that things are beginning to escalate. That is when it is best to switch strategies from defending our point of view to listening and using LEG. Some may feel at first that using this strategy makes them weak, but really the opposite is true. Consider Jesus' words in the Beatitudes:

'Blessed are the meek, for they will inherit the earth. …
Blessed are the merciful, for they will be shown mercy. …

Blessed are the peacemakers, for they will be called the children of God.'

MATTHEW 5:5, 7, 9

People who quietly trust in God's sovereignty rather than trying to take justice into their own hands are what Scripture calls 'meek'. This is not the same as weakness. It is, instead, strength that trusts in God and waits on his timing to work things out. It is humility and gentleness towards others, rather than power-grabs, coercion or control. Do not become a doormat, but be a peacemaker. Choose mercy.

If our long-term goal is to maintain a positive relationship with the person with whom we are in a heated discussion, then we should act on our God-given values with gentle conviction and kindness. The last part of LEG – the G – involves setting a Goal to address the problem that may involve some level of compromise, but within limits that do not lead to a violation of our faith, boundaries or values. This is where we assert our strength, but in the context of having connected and empathized with the other person.

If that sounds like hard work, you're right – it is. It may be a lot easier at times to just end the relationship. By choosing a skilful communication strategy to help nurture the relationship, we are bringing our strength under control when the person we may be in an argument with is not. We are taking responsibility for the relationship and attending to our need to maintain our own integrity at the same time.

However, please remember that it is still healthy to have limits. If LEG fails to help the other person begin to regulate, and the argument escalates to the point that it becomes abusive, it is better to lovingly disengage and have a cooling down period before returning to the discussion. De-escalation strategies will be discussed more fully in the pages ahead.

WRITE AND REFLECT

Think of a time when someone you know became upset. Instead of defending your position, or trying to make your point, how could switching to a LEG communication strategy have helped the other person cool down while preserving the relationship?

Write one sentence for each letter of the acronym LEG – keep it short and simple:

L - Listen What was the underlying God-given, basic human need that the other person had in the heated situation?

E - Endorse Without violating your own values, how could you have affirmed that the need was important?

G - Goal What are you willing and able to do to help the other person get their valid need met?

ASKING FOR WHAT YOU WANT

Again, it would be wonderful if we could just ask people for what we wanted, and they would never get upset or take offence. Unfortunately, this is not always the case. There may be certain times when we are afraid to ask for what we want because we fear rejection and/or an aggressive response.

In such cases, it may be wise to rehearse our request to improve our chances that the person we are asking will grant it, or at least meet us halfway. The acronym to remember for such a situation is IPA WIN:

- **Issue**: Describe the issue in a nutshell. Stick to facts at this point, not your feelings or opinions.
- **Perspective**: Once you've done that, it's time to share what you think or feel about it.
- **Assert**: Tell the other person what you want in a calm, kind tone.
- **WIN**: Describe how getting what you want will be win-win for both of you. Be willing to negotiate or compromise. If appropriate, you might consider asking the other person to pray about, or at least think about, your request.

WRITE AND REFLECT

Is there something you would like to ask for, but are afraid you will upset the person you are asking? Use IPA WIN to give your request the best possible chance of a favourable reception. Again, keep it short – one sentence for each part of the acronym:

I - Issue What is the issue? Stick to the facts.

P - Perspective How do you feel about it? What is your opinion?

A - Assert What do you want? Make your request using a kind tone.

INTRA-DEPENDENCY, BOUNDARIES AND LIMITS

Boundaries are typically thought of as lines between one thing and another that separate the two. Such lines are drawn to let us know where we begin and other people end, and vice versa. What is ours, versus what is somebody else's, helping us know what is, or isn't, our responsibility.

However, if we are entangled in the manner in which social theorists and quantum physicists have described (which we covered in Chapter 1), then our boundary delineations may not be as sharp as some suggest. This is not to take away from the idea that it is possible to protect ourselves from being taken advantage of, threatened or otherwise forced to do things that violate our values and beliefs or lead us away from our goals.

To the contrary, the intra-connectedness of people makes it possible to influence others through what we choose to accept or reject in others' behaviour. What we allow will come to matter, and what we don't, won't. In other words, what we do, or don't do, what we choose or leave out, has as much to do with who and what we are as it does with those around us.

Christ-followers are all connected with one another, forming the body of Christ which is meant to be intra-dependent. Each of us has been given gifts, and those gifts are meant to be used to build one another up into the fullness of Christ. God is in this mix too: he convicts, directs and intra-connects us all to one another as we pray, read Scripture and follow promptings that we receive from him.

Our intra-dependency at a local, material level is also readily apparent. People depend upon one another – police, teachers, grocers, truck drivers, employers, doctors, legislators, children and parents, etc. – to all do their part so that society works the way it is meant to work.

Expanding our view from local to global, it's clear that what happens in one community affects what happens in the nation, and what one nation does affects the others. Even the physical environment comes into play – with the air quality, global temperature and fabric of our atmosphere all eliciting a response from politicians and policymakers who write laws that affect us all.

Thus, we are all, in a very real sense, *intra*-dependent on a global scale. It is not just the swirling of thoughts, feelings and behaviours and the other people in your past or present that are intra-dependent and constitutive, it is all of us together, intra-acting within the world. We are all part of one large system, and all of us affect one another through chain reactions of behaviour across time and space that are all part of the dynamic becoming of the world.[20]

Even when we establish a boundary with someone, their behaviour will continue to affect us and those around us. It may force us to leave them, or stop giving them something, involve other people to get help, or tell them 'no' which may have

20 Barad, *Meeting the Universe Halfway.*

consequences. Because we are intra-connected and cannot help but shape and affect one another and the world around us, our responsibility is underscored and our response-ability is called upon.

For example, Scripture commands us to be gracious with each other; but the question in any given situation is, what is grace? Given that we are intra-connected, is it gracious of you to ignore someone else's destructive behaviour time and time again? Remember, your decision matters, and comes to be matter. How will your willingness to look the other way affect them? You? Others?

Or does grace mean establishing limits that protect me or others from someone's harmful behaviour, which may also encourage that person to change and grow, even if the process is difficult or time-consuming? These questions are also intricately connected with issues of morality and ethics. As we make and begin drawing boundaries or setting limits, we must ask ourselves who wins and who loses. What are we stopping, starting, rewarding, ignoring or punishing? What are the consequences for us and others?

There is a line between grace and the enablement of harmful behaviour, and the answer to which one is which may not always be obvious. But since we are intra-dependent on one another and response-able to one another, we have a spiritual, moral and ethical obligation to lovingly confront, rather than enable, destructive behaviour (as we define it).

GUIDING OUR DECISIONS

Here are a few principles that can guide our decisions when it comes to responses that facilitate change.[21] It is important to:

21 Dr Henry Cloud, Dr John Townsend, *Boundaries: When to Say Yes, When to Say No, To take Control of Your Life* (Zondervan, 1992).

- identify certain things that you will not do anymore (boundaries)
- identify things that you will only allow to a certain extent (limits)
- identify things that you will start doing (goals).

Note that setting a boundary or limit never seeks to control another person. Your 'boundaries' should only describe *your* actions: what you won't do, where you won't go, etc. Your 'limits' should describe things you will allow or participate in, but only up to a point. Your 'goals' should describe things that *you* want to start doing – not what you want others to start doing. What other people do is up to them, yet it is up to you to decide how you will respond to their choices.

If someone in our lives doesn't want to change their destructive behaviour, we can't force them. However, we don't have to facilitate it either. We can, for example, stop making excuses for them, stop keeping their behaviour a secret or stop funding their habits. By choosing to stop facilitating or enabling the destructive choices of others, we protect our own integrity and may influence them to change as they experience the natural consequences of their behaviour. This concept is put to good use by both secular and Christian writers of popular books on parenting.[22]

As we make careful decisions about what behaviours, attitudes and demands we will accept, limit or reject from one another (as guided by biblical principles) we are cooperating with the work of the Holy Spirit in our own lives and in the lives of others whose lives are entangled with ours. It is not helpful (or realistic) to tell someone else what they can or can't do – people will do what they want to do, unless they are enticed, or threatened, to do otherwise. But even if they are somehow incentivized to do

---

22 Foster Cline, *Parenting with Love and Logic: Teaching Children Responsibility* (Navpress, 1990); Danny Silk, *Loving Our Kids on Purpose* (Destiny Image Incorporated, 2016).

something they wouldn't normally do, if they don't develop the intrinsic desire to change at some point, they will revert back to their old behaviour as soon as the pressure is off, or there is nothing more to gain. This is one of the key principles of a secular therapy known as Motivational Interviewing.[23]

However, it is encouraging to know that just because we can't control the behaviour of others doesn't mean that we aren't influencing it. Because people are intra-connected, when one person who is part of a group of people (such as a family, church or community) changes, it will necessarily affect other people in the group.

Here's an example of what this might look like in real life: if you want to become healthier, you may decide not to eat fried food any more, or even go out to eat at a pub or restaurant that has fried food so that you will not be tempted. However, it would be overstepping to try to decide that since you are no longer eating fried food or visiting pubs, no one in your family should either.

It might be great if your family decided to get fitter together, but even though you have good motives, banning them from fried food when they want to keep eating it would be you (attempting to) impose your boundaries, goals and values upon them. Unless they are intrinsically motivated to stop eating fried food themselves, you'll have to establish a system of rewards or punishments to keep them motivated. If they never come to see the value in staying away from fried food, they will begin eating it again as soon as they can get away with it.

It is possible, though, that others in your family will get inspired when they see you getting fit and healthy, establishing new rhythms of sleep, grocery shopping and exercise. The great benefits of your success may help them develop the intrinsic motivation they need to make healthy changes in their own lives, and they may begin to take action.

23 William R Miller, Stephen Rollnick, *Motivational Interviewing: Helping People Change* (Guilford Press, 2013).

Or, they may not ... at least not easily. In fact, when one person's healthy change affects the whole system of people and status quo to which they are connected, they may encounter intense resistance. Unhealthy systems don't often change overnight, and old habits die hard. The person who wants to stop eating fried food may be tempted when one of their family members brings home a bucket of fried chicken for dinner!

If the system we are entangled with proves resistant to change, it may take some thought – and perhaps a bit of trial and error – to find a way to maintain changes even in an environment that is resistant to those changes.

In fact, sometimes people have a hard time changing themselves because they are enmeshed in a system that is very unhealthy – perhaps even destructive or abusive. In these cases, people may have to make some hard choices to ensure that, as far as it depends on them, they can develop a healthier life that is both compatible with their values and beliefs *and* safe. They may need to leave their home for a while, perhaps permanently, in order to establish and strengthen healthy life practices.

Such a person may need to involve the police, move into a safe house, get some financial help and/or join a support group. In this way, the decision of the abused person to seek help enables them to grow and becomes sedimented into who they are – it becomes part of their story. As people help them, and they gain independence and see that they are worthy of love and respect, and capable of earning a living, they will come to believe more and more that they are inherently valuable regardless of what their abuser told them. And part of being valuable means being worthy of setting limits on the types of behaviour you will or will not accept from others.

In the same way, because of intra-connectedness, their abuser will be forced to confront the relational, emotional, social and legal consequences of their behaviour. The self-insight they develop through this process, or the consequences of running away from problems, will equally become sedimented within them – it will become part of their story – either of confession and redemption, or of a continued hard-heartedness and the consequences of fleeing accountability.

People in recovery programmes learn to become skilled at setting limits, boundaries and goals for themselves. Not just to stop using their substances or engaging in unhealthy behaviours, but in all areas of their life. For them, and for all of us really, it is important to understand that whatever sorts of things we are involved in that are unhealthy or unhelpful affect us as a whole person. These are not compartmentalized events or activities. What we do, or don't do, affects us and others. It shapes us and becomes part of us in either helpful or unhelpful ways. Malik's story below illustrates this principle:

Malik

Writing a definition of sobriety, and the boundaries associated with it, helped me. I realized that if I was constantly breaking my boundaries then maybe I was not as 'sober' as I would like to be. Eventually, some of these boundaries, and some new goals, became my new definition of sobriety.

I no longer engage in the behaviours that came with my sexual addiction. I have gone through several phases of sobriety and have acted out twice since 28 February 2010, with my longest clean run being sixteen months. I have come to realize that what I considered sober then is not what I consider sober now. Sobriety now is much more narrowly defined than when I started. Each time that I acted out was actually because I allowed inappropriate material in, resulting in a slow downhill slide that ultimately led to a break in sobriety. Each break was necessary as the levels of 'denial' that I wrap myself in are creative and cunning.

Each break, though painful, has eventually led me to further enlightenment regarding the dangers of the world and the effect they have on a man driven to follow God's plan.

I no longer compare myself to others as it relates to my career, status, money and possessions. These were my idols, my false gods. One time in a teaching, the question was asked: 'What is your God?' and the answer was given: 'Anything that can ruin your day.' Pursuit of these idols definitely ruined my day more than once. I have come to realize that they only led to disappointment, increased pressure to perform, anger, resentment, bitterness and depression. All those repressed feelings fuelled arguments, separated me from my kids and kept me away from home.

The greatest change in my life since starting recovery has been with my wife. I no longer disparage her. Instead I accept her and do not judge her. I don't focus on other people's physical relationships with their wives, nor do I discuss mine and my wife's physical relationship with others or compare her to others. Instead, I look at her as perfect for me. Not many women would have stayed with me and I know now that she was divinely chosen for me, and that I need to treat her that way. My goal is to treat her with trust and respect.

I am also sharing my life as it revolves around church with others. I have a purpose and a function; service helps me to get to it. Once I dived into service and filled my life with the ministries of the Church, my whole demeanour and topics of conversation began to change. I slowly began to view the world in a very different way. Instead of constantly joking and using sexual innuendos, I now talk about father-son campouts, children's ministry, celebrate recovery, prayer ministry, LifeCare and summer Bible clubs for kids – I even went on an international mission trip where I got to share my story with other people struggling with a variety of issues.

Service has been a great joy for me. As I mentioned, I joined the prayer ministry. I never liked praying with others before. It felt weird and made me very uncomfortable. But when asked to join, I felt myself being guided by the Holy Spirit and knew that I had to respond with a 'Yes.' Serving in this ministry I found that I got to share my testimony with people and that front line prayer was very invigorating.

One Sunday, 3 June 2012, a woman I had prayed with and brought to recovery came up to me and thanked me. She told me that when I shared my past sins related to adultery, pornography, alcohol and drug addiction it helped her to feel comfortable enough to share her story. God used that to bring her into recovery and improve her life. She told me that I changed her life forever and that she is proud of me. She said that she thinks of me as the 'man in the orange shirt'. She said that she was led to me. During the service she felt compelled to go to 'the man in the orange shirt'. That Sunday represents one of the best days of my life.

I now have faith. I have burned the bridge and there is no turning back.

WRITE AND REFLECT

What limits do you need to establish in your life? These are things that you will not do. You cannot control other people, but you can decide what you will no longer do or be a part of. Start by simply making a choice or two about what you will no longer do or allow others to do to you. If your choices affect someone else, you might consider communicating them ahead of time, or easing into the changes.

SETTING GOALS

Usually it is not enough to simply stop doing something. People also need to start doing something new that will take the place of the old, unhealthy behaviours. That is often the key to sustainable change.

For instance, in the example we are using of a person deciding to get healthy – they may decide, 'I will keep the fridge stocked with healthy food so that when my family wants fast food, I will have an alternative waiting for me at home.' A healthy meal at home replaces an unhealthy meal at the pub.

This example contains several key elements that are important when setting goals, which are described below. A good acronym that can be used to remember the key elements of an attainable goal is COSMIC.

COSMIC GOALS

Is the plan:

- *Controllable?* Is this something that you have some control over? Are you able to achieve it regardless of what others do or don't do? Or, does it involve making others do things they have not agreed to do, or not do?
- *Obtainable?* Is it realistic and achievable?
- *Simple?* Is it broken down into small, specific tasks and goals?
- *Measurable?* Is progress observable and behavioural, rather than subjective and hard to quantify?
- *Immediate?* Are the conditions right to begin now?
- *Consistent?* Is it something you are committed to maintaining over time?

When making a plan for change, try setting goals that are COSMIC, and remember to break big goals down into several little goals. For example, a goal of going for a daily run might be broken down into small achievable goals, such as getting running shoes, planning a route, scheduling your run or starting off by walking instead of running. Big changes all at once may not be realistic or even achievable. And, if you fail, you may lose hope and give up altogether.

A less risky strategy is to set and achieve small goals over time. Attaining each goal becomes a reward and incentive to set and reach the next goal. Sometimes people refer to this strategy as 'pacing', or viewing life as a marathon rather than a sprint.

WRITE AND REFLECT

What goals would you like to set for yourself? Remember, goals are things that *you* do. You cannot control other people, so don't make your goals dependent on the (forced) participation or cooperation of others who have not agreed to help. Start with just a couple of new goals. If your goals will affect someone else, or change the dynamic of your family or group, I suggest communicating to them ahead of time to give others a chance to adjust. Or you might slowly ease into the changes, rather than making a radical shift.

DE-ESCALATION

We've all been there. Something happens that causes a minor disagreement; then somehow, the minor disagreement turns into a major argument. Both people begin defending their point of view, neither feels heard or understood, tempers flare and words spoken in anger are hard to take back later. Small disagreements can quickly escalate into relationship-killing fights.

De-escalation strategies can short-circuit this pattern before it begins. The problem is that it takes discipline to stop a disagreement from becoming destructive. That's because, usually, by the time it gets destructive, feelings are getting hurt and the desire to defend or attack can be very strong.

Imagine that you are on a raft, floating down a river. You hear the roar of a waterfall and know that if you wait too long to paddle to shore, the current will be too strong and it will carry you over the edge. The only sensible thing to do is paddle to shore when you are still far enough upstream that the current isn't yet too strong.

Similarly, when a person is in a disagreement and they sense it is getting too heated, they can do their part to de-escalate it. How?

- This may mean asking for a 'time-out' or 'recess' from the conversation.
- This can work well if the other person in the relationship is agreeable to the idea.
- It is important to note that the person calling the time-out should be the one to own their need for the time out. 'I'm getting upset and need some time to calm down,' is more likely to be effective than, 'You're yelling at me, I need a time out.'

If the other person is unwilling to stop the conversation, it may be because they experience the time-out as a painful abandonment or emotional disconnection. In this case, it may be more effective to stay connected and try using some of the communication techniques described earlier in this Chapter: LEG to help the other person cool down, and IPA WIN to ask for what you want. These strategies help you care for the other person and nurture the relationship, without diminishing your own value or compromising your integrity.

Whether due to a mental health issue, past trauma or simply a problem with rage, the other person may want to control or dominate you. They may use anger, threats and fear, or a sense of obligation, shame or guilt to intimidate you into staying connected with them in the argument. In such cases:

- you may have to leave the room in order to get away from them. Their anger, threats and unkind words may escalate; but this will be less damaging than staying and remaining in the destructive conversation;
- by using this strategy consistently, and being firm about it, in time the person you are in conflict with will see that their intimidation tactics don't work, and they will hopefully begin respecting your freedom to choose what behaviour you will or will not accept.

Another more diplomatic approach may be to allow distractions to enter the conversation:

- Answering the phone when it rings, turning off the laundry buzzer, or attending to a child in the next room may be just enough of a break to let emotions settle and give you time to think or pray.

These de-escalation strategies do come with a warning, however. If 'time-outs' are consistently used to avoid resolving an issue, the other person in the fight will become less and less willing to abide by them.

When both parties have had a chance to calm down, it is vital that time be made to discuss the topic and try to resolve it. Again, IPA WIN and LEG can be very helpful in this regard, giving us a framework with which to make requests of others, and in giving us a framework to hear and validate the other person, which can help them calm down.

By using these strategies in combination with one another as appropriate, all the time remembering your innate worth and value as a human being and child of God (no matter what the other person says about you or does to you), you will be able to craft an effective de-escalation and conflict-solving strategy. Remember that it is OK for you to take a break or seek help if you need it. And, over time, both parties will come to trust that when a time-out is called, the issue will still eventually be addressed and resolved.

WRITE AND REFLECT

When are you likely to need a de-escalation strategy? Which topics or relationships tend to be most turbulent in your life?

Would LEG, IPA WIN or some combination of the two, work for you?

What other concepts or strategies that you have learned so far in this book would help you navigate this relationship?

ABUNDANT LIFE

When I have promised my patients help or improvement by means of a cathartic treatment I have often been faced by this objection: 'Why, you tell me yourself that my illness is probably connected with my circumstances and the events of my life. You cannot alter these in any way. How do you propose to help me, then?' And I have been able to make this reply: 'No doubt fate would find it easier than I do to relieve you of your illness. But you will be able to convince yourself that much will be gained if we succeed in transforming your hysterical misery into common unhappiness. With a mental life that has been restored to health you will be better armed against that unhappiness.'

SIGMUND FREUD[24]

'I have told you these things, so that in me you may have peace. In this world you will have trouble. But take heart! I have overcome the world.'

JESUS (JOHN 16:33 NIV)

BUILDING UPON HOPE

Freud and Jesus both acknowledged that people face painful circumstances in life. Freud's strategy was to help people transition out of hysteria and into a more reasonable approach to

---

24 Sigmund Freud, 'The Psychotherapy of Hysteria from Studies on Hysteria' in *The Standard Edition of the Complete Psychological Works of Sigmund Freud, Vol II (1893–1895): Studies on Hysteria, 253-305*, p.304.

problems in living. As an atheist, that was the limit of what he had to offer. Though devoid of transcendent hope, his approach was pragmatic from a worldly perspective. Indeed, recent research in the field of positive psychology has taught us that building positive resources for emotional and physical health can act as 'shock absorbers' to help people deal more constructively with adversity and pain.[25]

A biblical worldview would not conflict with this approach in some respects, but certainly would go beyond it. Jesus offers hope that a day will come when what wasn't made right in this world will be made right in the next. On that day, what we suffer will be redeemed. The pain will be gone and the tears wiped away. We will be reunited with those we've lost. On that day, the senseless will be made clear, and we will bask in the ever-increasing glory of our Lord and Saviour.

Researchers have found that a sense of transcendent purpose – something bigger than oneself – is an important component of the good life.[26] Pascal thought and wrote about this same concept over 400 years ago; though, importantly, he had come to believe that the irreplaceable, transcendent cause that gave life meaning and purpose was God:

> ... *there was once in man a true happiness of which there now remains to him only the mark and empty trace, which he in vain tries to fill from all his surroundings, seeking from things absent the help he does not obtain in things present. But these are all inadequate, because the infinite abyss can only be filled by an infinite and immutable object, that is to say, only by God Himself.*

BLAISE PASCAL, *PASCAL'S PENSÉES*

We are hard-wired for God, with eternity in our hearts. Strive though we might to replace him, millions, even billions, have found that nothing else compares.

25 Roko Belic, Eiji Han Shimizu, Frances Reid, Vivien Hillgrove, Mark Adler, and Marci Shimoff, *Happy* (2012).
26 Viktor E. Frankl, *Man's Search for Meaning: An Introduction to Logotherapy* (Boston Press, 1992).

And yet, in the absence of a relationship with God, people are driven to seek something bigger than themselves with which to ward off the spectre of their own existential insignificance. Some find their transcendent purpose in environmentalism, social justice or their children. However, if indeed there is no life after death, no world beyond this one, then such causes can only be enveloped within an overall purposelessness. When the last human is gone, or the sun explodes and vaporizes our galaxy, whatever transcendent purpose they have constructed and invested in will go with them. They will have provided nothing more than temporary meaning within an eternal meaninglessness.

For some, that is perhaps enough, or at least, all there is to be had when the cold hard truth is faced. Indeed, if God is not real, and Jesus is not his Son who is fully God and fully human, then Christianity is just another false construct – at worst, a construct that serves to limit our freedom, rather than give it. The Apostle Paul agreed, writing, 'If only for this life we have hope in Christ, we are of all people most to be pitied' (1 Corinthians 15:19 NIV).

Yet if the God of Scripture exists, then Jesus offers something more. An opportunity to intra-act with him, to build an eternal kingdom, which starts in our hearts and works its way out from there, influencing our thoughts, actions, emotions, relationships, the discourse of the social world and all creation around us. What a high calling for this life! But it doesn't end there. We also have hope in the next life. This is, on the face of it, an incredible resource that Christians can avail themselves of as they await solutions that may yet be a long way off for the problems of today.

You can build on this hope. It is the reason to carry on even when you are in 'the valley of the shadow of death' (Psalm 23:4 ESV). You can trust that he is working things out and has a plan. Part of that plan may be for you to learn how to add positive activities into your routine as he provides the people and opportunities to make it happen. Consider joining that group you heard about. Begin investing in relationships that are important to you. Contribute to that cause you're passionate about. Chase that dream you've always had. Volunteer at church or in your community – perhaps by doing something that is related to the very issue or challenge that you yourself are facing. While you're waiting on God's timing for the bigger, more painful issues in your life to be resolved, these resources and positive activities can end up being a massive conduit through which God brings you comfort and strength – and perhaps does the same for others through you.

HEALTHY LIVING

In the movie *Chariots of Fire*, Scottish Olympic champion and Christian missionary Eric Liddell, says, 'God made me fast. And when I run, I feel his pleasure.'[27] What is it that you do that gives you a sense of God's pleasure? Whatever it is, find it and get involved in whatever capacity you are willing and able.

HEARTS is a tool to help us remember the components of a healthy life, balanced with purpose, relationship and joy. No one disputes that these are good things to get involved in – they are compatible with both Scripture and recent research in psychotherapy and positive psychology research:

- Hobbies - the arts, reading, social or political activism.
- Exercise - sports, working out, 'flow' activities.[28]
- Affection - healthy touch and relationships, being around people who bring joy and comfort.
- Rest - regular sleep, relaxation and respite.
- Time for yourself - believe you're worth it – budget time for and schedule self-care activities.
- Spiritual Activities - worship, service, church, Scripture, prayer, gratitude for blessings in life.

27 Hugh Hudson, *Chariots of Fire* (Allied Stars Ltd, 1981).
28 A very interesting read is *Flow* by Mihaly Csikszentmihalyi. However, this book comes with a warning that it is written from an atheistic worldview that can be disturbing to people of faith. If you do not have a familiarity with apologetics or embrace the challenge of defending the faith from critics, I do not recommend it.

Look for ways to develop in areas where there is low-hanging fruit. In other words, look for activities and groups that you can plug into easily that will make your life better now. Sometimes we can get so focused on our problems that we fail to recognize some of the great things we could add into our lives while those problems are being resolved. Remember to break down big goals into small, easier to achieve goals first.

I would also encourage you to explore the groups your church and broader community have to offer. While group participation can be challenging or intimidating, it is worth trying. If you can find a healthy group, you will find that they can help you in ways that you cannot do alone, and give you more resources to draw from in times of acute need – as well as giving you a place where you can serve and contribute to others.

Mike

I knew that something else was missing … service. You see, at one point in my life, I had actually taught in church. I had been 'in the ballgame', leading and teaching, but I had taken myself out. I was satisfied just going to meetings and soaking it in. But God had other plans.

'What God? You want me to tell my story? You want me to share? To lead? That would mean I would have to open my soul.'

Remember, I did not have a very high opinion of myself before, let alone after the mess I had made of my life. So putting myself out there was not very high on my list. I was believing the lies of the enemy. My recovery partner shared with me that we are all soldiers who had been wounded. And although wounded soldiers do need to rest, they also need to get back to the fight. So I started leading, first in small groups and then through some teaching.

That was what was missing in my life. I needed to get back to the fight. I needed to share my story. Not because it was so special or had some great significance, but because that was what God wanted me to do, to be obedient to him.

Through this time, God showed me how to go through problems, not around them. You see, before when a struggle would come to me, I would check out, either through drugs, alcohol or whatever. This is the same coping mechanism I used as a child. When bad things would happen, or I was afraid, I went to my room and shut the door. I did the same thing as an adult, I just used substances, or other things to be by myself.

Now I have come to realize that God has a plan for all my trials and tribulations (James 1:1–4). God wants me to go through the trial, not around it. God wants me to learn and grow. I was cheating myself out of a valuable life lesson by not using my struggles to help others.

Finally, I've come full circle. I have allowed God to dictate my life in many ways, and he has truly blessed me. He has given me back almost everything I lost (Joel 2:25). I am now working as a physician again and have a great practice. I am remarried to a wonderful woman, my kids are doing well, I am leading a study for others with struggles and I am sharing my story. I am also seeking a way to create or join a group for other physicians struggling with issues that could threaten their practice. I give all the honour and glory to God.

WRITE AND REFLECT

Look through the HEARTS list. What can you add to your life to bring you some peace and joy, even whilst you are working on other problematic areas of your life? Consider a goal of adding at least one positive resource into your regular routine. Or if that's too much, how about a goal of getting information about one or two new groups each month, so that you can pray about whether God is leading you to attend and participate?

CONNECTING TO COMMUNITY

No man is an island,
Entire of itself,
Every man is a piece of the continent,
A part of the main.

JOHN DONNE, 'FOR WHOM THE BELL TOLLS'

Bonnie

In my group at church I could voice my hurts and struggles. I asked someone to work with me – they call it a sponsor – she was safe and non-judgmental. She gave me options I could try or keep in mind for when I found myself facing tough circumstances or confrontation, which used to be triggers for me to want to control things, become critical or drink. For example: speak truth in love, walk blamelessly, set healthy boundaries and meet the legitimate needs of others. Rest in God, trust in God and wait on God. She also gave me the suggestion to ask myself the question, 'What is my role?' when I am confused as to which course to take. I decided to try using these tools, and they have worked well for me.

I also found a non-judgmental accountability partner from the group who spoke truth where the enemy has spoken lies, which helped me find freedom from my anxiety. I learned that doing what it says to do in Philippians 4:8 – which says to fix our thoughts on things that are true, noble, right, lovely excellent and worthy of praise – helps me with my anxiety. When my mind starts wandering in fearful thoughts, I fix my thoughts on these things and I have peace.

I draw from these experiences now as I care for others in ministry, and in my daily life.

Sometimes, working through problems is a lot like trying to dig a hole in rocky soil. We need a pickaxe to break up the rock, and a shovel to scoop the rock and dirt out of the hole.

Going through these exercises with a pastor, mentor, coach, counsellor or some other person you trust is like the pickaxe because it can help us gain insight into tough issues that are blocking our progress. Peer support groups are like the shovel, because once we become aware of the tough issues, we can process them further by talking about the issues we have come to be aware of in a specialized group that is committed to supporting one another.

That's how community support and the LifeCare ministry work hand-in-hand. It is intra-action at its finest – a web of relationships for ongoing support, to offer a place to serve, and which will be there safely in place when temptation or difficult circumstances arise. That point is important. You don't put your seatbelt on in the middle of an accident. You put it on every time you get into the car, and you hope you don't need it; but if you do, it's there to prevent a bad situation from ending in trauma or even a tragic and unnecessary loss of life.

Many things that can be gained through participation in a group cannot be gained through one-to-one relationships and vice versa:

- People who have been hurt in the context of community often need to be healed in the context of community.
- A healthy experience of community gives people confidence in relationships and helps them see that they have something of value to contribute.
- Church involvement and support/recovery groups can provide expert information about an area of struggle.
- Groups are often less expensive and more accessible than professional help.
- Relating to peers who have been 'in your shoes' can be less intimidating than relating to a single professional carer.

- Groups can give you a place to serve and find meaning in your most painful experiences.
- There are church or community-based resources that can help meet your needs for food, clothing, shelter and safety. When basic human needs go unmet, it is not possible to work on higher emotional needs.[29]
- Even in secular community groups, there are ways to express and share your faith as you work towards social justice.

Advice before you join a group

You should not join a group until you feel ready to function within it. Be choosy about the groups you join. Do some research. Ask about the rules of the group. If the group dynamic leads to pressure to perform in a way you are not yet ready for, it could lead to an increase in feelings of guilt or shame for not measuring up. You may choose to deal with this pressure in unhealthy ways that you will keep hidden from the group to avoid the risk of feeling judged or rejected. For example, rather than admit that they are struggling in some way to regulate emotionally, people may sometimes revert to self-harming behaviours, or relapse on a substance after group time is over, to escape painful feelings.

If you join a group and it appears to be having a negative effect on you, consider exploring whether the group is a good fit. While groups are wonderful, everything has its season, and it may just not be the right time. Another group may be better suited for your needs, or you may need more one-to-one time with someone you trust so that you can build up more internal resources before you are ready to join a group.

29 Kendra Cherry, 'The Five Levels of Maslow's Hierarchy of Needs', *verywellmind*, http://psychology.about.com/od/theoriesofpersonality/ss/maslows-needs-hierarchy_5.htm#step-heading (Accessed 15 November 2018).

But I'm not comfortable in groups

People often tell me that they don't want to join a support or recovery group because they are not comfortable in groups. When I ask why, they tell me that listening to other people's problems causes them stress or anxiety, and they feel this makes them more likely to relapse into old patterns of behaviour in order to get some relief. I can't tell you how many times I've heard, 'I didn't feel like I needed a drink when I went to the group, but after listening to those people's stories, I sure wanted one when I came out!' or, 'I've got enough problems of my own without listening to everyone else's!' or, 'I can't stop thinking about their problems and wanting to fix them.'

I get it. People have been through some hard things; and, if you're an empathetic person, and prone to taking on other people's problems as your own, listening to others in a support group can be stressful. If that is how you feel, then I would ask you to consider the following:

- Isolation and a lack of healthy accountability is often a precursor to relapse.
- Being hurt by people in unhealthy groups in the past may be influencing your feelings about a group in the present that you are considering joining. If that is the case, take it slow. Realize that this new group is different from the unhealthy group you were part of in the past. Perhaps you could have a new experience in this group that could help heal the lingering pain of past group participation.
- Realize that while being part of a group does mean listening to and supporting others during group time, it definitely does not mean that their struggles are your responsibility to fix. Your job in a group will often be limited to offering information, prayer, encouragement, a listening ear and your own story from which others can draw insights into their own struggles as God leads them. And their job is to do the same for you.

- When group members share details about their lives, listen with an ear to hear what God is showing you about yourself. Even when people have different struggles, there are often similar dynamics you can apply to your situation. At the least, their story will provide insight that helps you better relate to others going through similar things.

WRITE AND REFLECT

Is there a group that you can join that will help you achieve your goals, maintain your boundaries and give you access to resources that will help you get where you would like to go in life? Consider doing some research if you're not sure. Search the web. Ask a pastor, friend, counsellor, doctor or psychologist. If you can find a group, set a goal to make contact with them and visit at least once. Use the space here to take notes on groups you know about or are interested in researching:

CHAPTER 12

ATTENDING TO RELATIONSHIPS

The people who were the most satisfied in their relationships at age 50 were the healthiest at age 80.

ROBERT WALDINGER, DIRECTOR OF THE HARVARD STUDY
OF ADULT DEVELOPMENT[30]

YOUR RELATIONAL HEALTH

In Chapter 5, during the Personal History Journal exercise, you bravely identified relationships with others that were damaged. However, we have waited until now to address those hurts. That was done on purpose because working on relationships can be very hard work. But, as Robert Waldinger suggests, relational health is very important. In fact, if the conclusions of the Harvard study he directs have any merit, then it is perhaps the most important thing we can invest in. This is yet another example of how the way we choose to intra-act with others (with hatred and resentment, or with love and forgiveness) actually begins to define the health of our physical bodies.

Of course, Jesus also had something to say on the topic of our relationships and their importance. As usual, he cuts right to the heart of the matter, and doesn't ask us to do anything he hasn't been willing to do himself.

---

30 Robert Waldinger cited by Liz Mineo, 'Harvard study, almost 80 years old, has proved that embracing community helps us live longer, and be happier', *The Harvard Gazette*, 11 April 2017, https://news.harvard.edu/gazette/story/2017/04/over-nearly-80-years-harvard-study-has-been-showing-how-to-live-a-healthy-and-happy-life/ (Accessed 15 November 2018). The Harvard Study of Adult Development has tracked the health and happiness of a cohort of 268 men for over eighty years.

Now when the Pharisees heard that he had silenced the Sadducees, they assembled together. And one of them, an expert in religious law, asked him a question to test him: 'Teacher, which commandment in the law is the greatest?' Jesus said to him, "'Love the Lord your God with all your heart, with all your soul, and with all your mind." This is the first and greatest commandment. The second is like it: "Love your neighbor as yourself." All the law and the prophets depend on these two commandments.'

MATTHEW 22:34–40

Forgiveness, amends and reconciliation are powerful tools that can help us in this God-given, research-supported goal of relational health.

However, before we proceed, I strongly suggest that you don't do this work alone if you have suffered significant stress at the hands of another, including but not limited to physical or sexual abuse. And, although we will discuss forgiveness in the pages ahead, I want to be very clear that forgiveness is something that you do for you, to find relief from anger and bitterness. And, forgiveness need not mean returning to a relationship with, or being vulnerable to, the person who harmed you. Forgiveness and reconciliation are not the same thing. I will explain this further as we go along.

Even for those who have suffered moderate abuse or stress, forgiveness, amends and reconciliation are often difficult. In twelve-step recovery programmes, the first wave of people to drop out do so at step four – the moral inventory – when people write down a list of those who have hurt them, those they have hurt, and a summary of the damage. The second wave usually happens in step five, when people are asked to share their inventory with their sponsor. And some of those who make it through those two difficult steps will drop out in steps six or seven, when people are asked to confront their feelings about those who have harmed them, or in steps eight and nine, when it is time to make amends with people they have harmed.

WHAT WE HAVE LEARNED SO FAR ...

By placing this chapter towards the end of the book, it is my hope that you have become ready to address this difficult area of life, having developed some new skills and resources to help support you in the process.

Let's review some of them now:

1. You have come to understand that your foundational value as a human being, made in God's image and worth enough to die for, coupled with your identity in Christ, gives you a spiritual basis upon which to begin to address or repair relationships in the past that have marked you in some unwanted way, or aren't working the way you want them to in the present.

2. You have gained insight into the intra-relations of the past that have moulded you, contributing to both your strengths and struggles.

3. If you have taken the step of sharing this journey with another, you will have gained an ally who knows you and with whom you can share difficult, personal things.

4. You have a way of identifying unwanted or unhelpful thoughts and changing them in order to change your feelings and behaviours.

5. You have identified ways of acting against your emotions to change the way you feel.

6. You have developed a list of activities that you can do when you are too stressed to think or use your other resources.

7. You have developed a set of problem-solving skills.

8. You have developed a set of measurable goals so that you can take the next step in becoming the person you want to be.

9. You have learned some communication skills that can help you ask for what you want in a skilful way or help someone else feel heard so that they can cool down when they are upset.

10. You have identified specialized groups that you can connect with for support.

MOVING ON: WITH FORGIVENESS AND RECONCILIATION

Armed with these resources, we now turn to forgiveness, reconciliation and amends, and to the difficult relationships in your life with which you may have some unfinished business.

If we have been forgiven when we didn't earn or deserve it, then the forgiveness we have found in Christ will give us yet another reason to forgive others who haven't earned or deserved it. Knowing that we are already forgiven by God, and that our intrinsic value is secure, may give us the confidence and motivation to make amends to those we have hurt – regardless of what we fear their response to us might be.

Unfortunately, forgiveness, amends and reconciliation are often misunderstood or poorly conceptualized by confused researchers and even biblical scholars. People confuse reconciliation with forgiveness or advocate unhelpful and unnecessary methods of forgiveness. As if this weren't bad enough, they often inappropriately use Scripture to lend credence and authority to their view, spiritualizing the process in a way that forces or guilts people into reconciling before the hard work is done by both parties to make true reconciliation possible. I don't want to overstate this, but such coercion borders on, and can quickly become, a form of spiritual abuse.

The biblical truth is that because forgiveness is not reconciliation, and need not involve the person who harmed us at all, forgiveness is possible. Even if we never speak to or see the person who harmed us ever again. It is often possible to make amends as long as the person who harmed us is safe to be around, appropriate to contact and still alive.

But it may not always be possible, or advisable, to reconcile. That is because for true reconciliation to occur, both parties in a conflict must be willing and able to do their part. The offending party must make complete amends, and the offended party must truly forgive. There are no shortcuts. And when one party isn't willing to engage in the process by being honest about their role in the conflict, reconciliation won't work. At best an uneasy détente can be struck, allowing the underlying problems in the relationship to lie dormant, waiting to be triggered and flare up again.

Understanding the difference between forgiveness, amends and reconciliation is essential if we are to discern the way to freedom from past or ongoing intra-relational damage. It is that subject to which we now turn.

FORGIVENESS

Deanna

What surprised me were the strong feelings that came with dropping my anger. Anger was an effective cover-up for pain and fear. When I couldn't be angry, I was left with those emotions.

It has been said that unforgiveness is like drinking poison and hoping your enemy will die, or that it is like allowing someone to rent space in your head for free.

Few deny the value of forgiveness. Current secular research advocates forgiveness as a means of relieving stress and anxiety, and acknowledges the role of forgiveness in resolving interpersonal conflict.[31] The Bible also emphasizes, in the strongest possible way, the importance of forgiveness (Matthew 18:21–35). Recovery programmes around the world focus on the role of forgiveness in step six, becoming ready for God to remove defects of character such as unforgiveness, and then in step seven, by asking him to remove these shortcomings by forgiving

---

31 Suzanne Freedman, 'Forgiveness and Reconciliation: The Importance of Understanding How They Differ' in *Counseling and Values* vol. 42 no. 3 (1998), pp.200–216.

through the empowering work of his word and Spirit.

But what forgiveness is exactly, what it means concretely, is often misunderstood. These misunderstandings lead people to dismiss the possibility of forgiveness, thinking that it demands too much of them. Much of this apprehension can be resolved by understanding what it really means to forgive. Therefore, to begin with, let's create a working understanding of forgiveness.

Forgiveness is:
- for you, not for them
- done between just you and God, and not necessarily offered directly to the offender, especially if they are unrepentant. Jesus did not look down from the cross and tell the people crucifying him that he forgave them. They were unrepentant and would only have mocked him. Instead he asked the Father (who was also himself) to forgive them. In other words, he himself is forgiving them. This principle makes it possible to forgive people who are no longer alive, who are not possible to visit, or who it would not be safe to be around
- turning the offending person over to God for judgment – taking them off your hook and putting them on God's
- something you do each time feelings of anger or bitterness over old hurts come up. You may need to forgive someone many times until feelings of bitterness or anger over old hurts go away
- something you do after every offence – but again, it is for you to cleanse yourself of anger and bitterness – not for them.

Forgiveness is not:
- saying that you want to return to relationship with the offending party
- something you offer to *get* something – for example

complete amends or even just a simple apology – as this may lead to disappointment and further pain if you forgive them but they do not make full amends

- saying that what was done was OK
- saying that what was done didn't hurt
- dependent on receiving an apology. If it were, the offending party would hold the only key to the chains of anger and bitterness that bind you. Don't wait to get an apology in order to forgive and be free!

Forgiving someone definitely does not mean that you must return to relationship with that person – especially if you think they are only going to continue hurting you in the same way. It is a form of spiritual abuse for someone to use Scripture to encourage you to return to a relationship where you will be vulnerable to someone who is unrepentant and likely to hurt you again physically, sexually or financially (for example, someone addicted to gambling who is driving you into debt).

We *can* forgive and even love someone (in the *agape* sense – a sort of general, universal love for others in our shared humanity (1 Corinthians 16:14)) without returning to a relationship with them where we are vulnerable. In fact, maintaining appropriate limits with such people may be the best way to love them, because it helps them to understand that their actions have consequences which God can use to bring them to a point of repentance and change.

It is also important to note that we can only forgive a hurt to the extent that we acknowledge it. If someone hurt us at a ten, on a pain scale of one to ten, but we are only willing to acknowledge that they hurt us at a three, then when we forgive them we are only forgiving thirty per cent of the offence. We can only forgive what we are able to acknowledge. Be honest about your feelings – not overplaying them, but not underplaying them either.

WRITE AND REFLECT

Drawing from the list you made in your Personal History Journal, who do you need to forgive to find freedom from past hurts? If you are having trouble forgiving, it may be helpful to start by just making the list of people you are holding anger, bitterness or resentment towards, knowing that you are not yet actually going to take them off your hook and put them onto God's. Instead, just make your list using the format below, then begin talking to God about your feelings towards the people who have hurt you. Another option is to begin talking about your feelings with someone you trust.

Remember, forgiving is not for-getting, it is for freedom!

The Person:

The Offence:

How it affected me then:

How it affects me now:

AMENDS

Remember, guilt is the feeling that we get when we have violated our own moral principles. If we feel guilty, but have not violated our own moral principles, then it is appropriate to act against the guilty feeling (as discussed in Chapter 9). This guilty feeling may have been engendered in us by others seeking to control our behaviour in a way that suited them. The classic example is the abused spouse who feels guilty for leaving or phoning the police after they have been assaulted.

If our guilt is due to having violated our own moral principles, however, then it is appropriate to first bring it to God. Remember that the penalty has already been paid for what we have done, so that our relationship with God will not be broken, nor our value diminished. Ever. No matter what. He will always forgive you, he loves you unconditionally and he will never leave you.

From this foundation of love and acceptance, we can make amends to the person we hurt knowing that even if they reject us and remain angry or mistrustful of us, God will always accept us, and we have not lost value in his sight. Moreover, the limit of our responsibility in the relationship is to make a complete amends as described below and begin to make changes in our lives accordingly, but that is where it ends. In the section ahead, we'll discuss what to do when we have made amends and the person we have harmed is unwilling to forgive.

That said, like forgiveness, amends is often misunderstood. It is not just a simple confession and apology. It is much more.

A complete amends has five parts:
- Confession: 'I did it.'
- Apology: 'I am sorry.'
- Empathy: 'I can understand how you might feel _____.'
- Repay or Repair: 'To make it up to you I will _____.'
- Commit to a change process to become safe and rebuild

trust over time: 'To prevent this from happening again, I will _____.' This is known in recovery circles as a 'living amends' – an ongoing change process that you begin to bring your behaviour into line with your values.

Sometimes people try to shortcut the amends process by confessing and apologizing, and then expecting, or even demanding forgiveness. People sometimes even use Scripture to try to force Christians to forgive them. I strongly urge you not to take this tack.

For example, 'I said I was sorry – doesn't the Bible say you have to forgive me if you're a Christian?' Or they might reference the parable of the unmerciful servant in Matthew 18 and say something like, 'Doesn't the Bible say that if you don't forgive me then God won't forgive you?'

Obviously, forgiveness is central to the gospel. Yet, if unforgiveness caused a follower of Christ to lose their salvation, then our salvation would be dependent on our good works. Such a position is not defensible in the context of Scripture as a whole, which makes it clear that our salvation is based on God's grace, not our good works. And, in the case of Matthew 18, the person who owed the debt to the unforgiving servant was repentant and willing to pay back what he owed. So, one might make the case that this parable is an example of an offended person who is unwilling to forgive someone who has made a full amends – at least, they acknowledged the debt (confession and apology) and were willing to work over time to repay the debt (repayment and commitment to change).

Using Scripture and biblical principles to guilt or shame someone into reconciliation with an unrepentant person is harmful – potentially even abusive. Even if we manage to elicit forgiveness from the person we harmed, there can be no reconciliation if complete amends (all five steps) has not been made. Forgiveness without amends can lead to the offended person being harmed again and again by the same destructive pattern of behaviour which has not been repented for and changed, thus initiating the well-known cycle of offence-apology-repeat that is prevalent in cases of abuse, addiction and chronic infidelity.

What's more, forgiveness without complete amends isn't effective or healthy even for the offender. It's only enablement (often in the name of grace) of behaviour that harms both the offender and offended alike by allowing the cycle to continue unchecked.

Change is hard work, and sometimes people continue to do the wrong thing even once they wholeheartedly understand it is wrong (a fuller discussion of the process of change is included in our LifeCare training seminars). The Apostle Paul struggled with that very issue regarding his 'thorn in the flesh' (2 Corinthians 12:7–10 NIV).

However, when a person is truly repentant and does commit the same offence again, they will make complete amends each time. Each time they fall back into old patterns they will make new amends, starting by confessing and moving through the process from there.

All that said, yes, God does command us to forgive. But he also commands us to make amends to people we have harmed and do our part to be reconciled to one another, as demonstrated in the verse below:

'Therefore, if you are offering your gift at the altar and there remember that your brother or sister has something against you, leave your gift there in front of the altar. First go and be reconciled to them; then come and offer your gift.'

MATTHEW 5:23–24 NIV

In this verse, the person offering their gift appears to be the offending party, as indicated by the description of the brother or sister having something against them. In this case, as the offender, it is their responsibility to go and make amends to the person they have harmed to do their part in affecting reconciliation. Whether or not the person they offended forgives them is beyond their control.

Deanna

My mum tried to rein me in with control and anger, but by my senior year there was only a shell of relationship left as I counted the days to leave for college. Now I have come to see that her attempts to control me were a form of love for her. She was worried about me and didn't know what else to do. I wish I could talk with her now and try to reconcile, but sadly she died of lung cancer in 2005. We barely spoke for the last three years of her life.

Mike

It was fairly easy to list my set of regrets, pains or resentments. The difficult part came in figuring out what my part was in all of it. Sometimes the most difficult person to get to know is the person in the mirror. My real breakthrough came in making amends with those I had hurt. As I shared before, my parents had passed away several years before, but I needed to tell them some things. I wrote a letter and read it at their headstones. I am not saying that is for everyone, but I will tell you that it was one of the most important milestones in my recovery.

Birdie

I also had to make amends to many people for my anger. I've hurt a lot of people with my anger. My words have had an enormous impact, I know. While I can be a great encourager, I know that over the years, I've also practised their use as a weapon. It was a hard moment when God gave me the wisdom to see that my words have the potential to kill a person's spirit. James 4:2 describes my anger struggle well, 'You desire but you do not have, so you kill. You covet but you cannot get what you want, so you quarrel and fight. ...' (NIV). When I did make amends to the people I've hurt in my anger, I was surprised that every single one of them was one hundred per cent gracious with me. That was more favour from the Lord.

WRITE AND REFLECT

Drawing from your Personal History Journal, who do you need to make amends to in order to begin rebuilding the relationship? It is important to point out that there may be some people who we have hurt that it would be inappropriate to contact (for example, someone with whom we had an adulterous or otherwise inappropriate relationship). If this is your situation, it will be helpful for you to share the issue with a LifeCarer, or some other person who you trust will keep what you share confidential.

As is the case in the process of forgiveness, if you are having trouble finding the courage to make amends, it may be helpful to start by just making the list of people you feel led to make amends to (which might even include you making amends with yourself), knowing that you don't yet have to actually approach anyone at this point. Instead, just make the list, then pray that God will help you to become willing to make amends and provide you with an opportunity when the time is right.

WHAT IF A NON-CHRISTIAN OFFENDER WON'T MAKE AMENDS?

Like us, non-Christians will consider their values when it comes to how they resolve relational conflict. It's just that their values may not be the same as ours. Sometimes, they may be very different. In fact, I personally have heard a non-Christian psychotherapy professor who holds a doctorate from a well-respected, internationally acclaimed university, advocate 'hate' as a method of protecting oneself from those who have harmed them. Because apparently, when we hate someone, we don't care about how they feel or even whether they live or die. Welcome to the dark side!

However, Matthew 18:15–17 provides some guidelines for conflict resolution for those in the Church, and it may also be helpful to those who do not hold Scripture as the highest authority in their lives.

In exploring these guidelines, it is important to note that the only biblical reason to confront someone with their hurtful behaviour, and any form of church discipline that may follow, is always, first and foremost, reconciliation. Not to punish, blame or shame the offending party.

That said, the process is first for the offended party to let the offender know they've hurt them. If the offender won't listen, the offended person is to get two or three witnesses to talk to the offender with them. Importantly, it is at this stage that both parties will have an opportunity to present their side of the story. People who hear the grievances of others would be wise to remember the Proverb,

In a lawsuit the first to speak seems right,
  until someone comes forward and cross-examines.

PROVERBS 18:17 NIV

If the offending party is at fault and unrepentant, then according to Matthew 18 they are to be treated as an unbeliever.

I take this to mean that the church now has some indication that perhaps the offending party is unrepentant because they do not fully understand the gospel. Treating them as an unbeliever is not a punishment, but rather is only that which is in keeping with their offending and unrepentant behaviour. They have effectively placed themselves outside the community of Christ-followers by not living according to the principles of that community, which in this case, is for an offender to make complete amends and seek reconciliation to restore unity.

Yet it is also very important to remember that Christians are called to not only love those who are their friends but are also called to love those who are their enemies (Matthew 5:43–47). The question then is: what does it mean to treat an unrepentant brother or sister as an unbeliever?

THE UNREPENTANT BROTHER OR SISTER

Now I urge you, brothers and sisters, to watch out for those who create dissensions and obstacles contrary to the teaching that you learned. Avoid them!

ROMANS 16:17

But if anyone does not obey our message through this letter, take note of him and do not associate closely with him, so that he may be ashamed. Yet do not regard him as an enemy, but admonish him as a brother.

2 THESSALONIANS 3:14–15

These verses must be read carefully, and in light of the whole of Scripture. As mentioned previously, the feeling of shame tells us that our behaviour will exclude us from the group. This seems to be the point of these verses – that the person who is engaging in behaviour that is not consistent with their faith should be given a clear signal that what they are doing is not OK.

They will begin to notice that members of the spiritual community will not associate 'closely' with them anymore. The verse in Thessalonians also makes a point to clarify, 'Yet do not regard him as an enemy, but admonish him as a brother.'

Some in the secular community use the phrase 'withdraw with love' to describe this way of avoiding someone you still love and are connected to, but whose behaviour is hurting you or others.

Dr Kevin McCauley is a specialist in addiction recovery who is in recovery himself. He notes that both airline pilots and physicians have addiction recovery groups for members of their profession. While some may come proactively, many are mandated to come, often during a leave of absence from work, while they attend to their recovery. They are 'brothers and sisters' in the profession who are being treated as outsiders – in the sense that they are not allowed to participate in their profession because they are impaired. However, for those who engage in the recovery process, the groups boast recovery and re-employment rates as high as ninety-seven per cent. Dr McCauley credits the success rate of these groups to an overall message of belonging (this group is for *us*), balanced with disapproval of the behaviour (*we* don't do that).[32]

Another secular researcher, Alan Jenkins, wrote:

> *We are inviting a man to embark upon a painful journey, which requires a readiness to carry the shame on his own shoulders. Such a journey inevitably requires entering a sense of disgrace which initially involves a negative judgment of self, but recognizing that atonement lies in these realizations, and taking steps to own and express them.*[33]

---

32 Kevin T. McCauley, M.D., 'Ten Tips for the First Year of Recovery', http://www.transforminglifecenter.com/wp-content/uploads/2015/07/TenTipsForFirstYearOfRecovery.pdf (Accessed 21 November 2018).
33 Alan Jenkins, 'Shame, Realisation and Restitution: The Ethics of Restorative Practice', *Australian and New Zealand Journal of Family Therapy, vol. 27* (3) (2013), pp.153-162.

It must be emphasized that a biblical approach is to judge the behaviour and not the whole person. However, it does seem that only when the offending party experiences an authentic sense of wrongdoing for their actions do they become truly repentant, make amends (which includes a life change) and seek reconciliation.

WRITE AND REFLECT

Is there someone who has hurt you and is not willing to make amends? Or perhaps they are unable to make amends because they have passed away or are unable to contact you for some other reason. How does their lack of repentance continue to affect your attitudes, behaviours and current relationships?

RECONCILIATION

This person who hurt me had never made amends to me. This has contributed to my continuing anger towards them.

LIFECARE TRAINING PARTICIPANT

My LifeCarer was so encouraging. I began to realize that though trust was still being rebuilt in this damaged relationship, everything that needed to happen for reconciliation to continue had happened, and I hadn't realized that before. It felt really good. She's also been really empathetic about difficult things I'm dealing with and I feel like she's just here for me – that's a nice feeling as well.

LIFECARE TRAINING PARTICIPANT

Armed with that information, we now turn to reconciliation itself. Reconciliation refers to a return to relationship. Not to the same broken relationship, but to a better, more mature relationship. For this to happen, the offended party must forgive, and the offending party must make complete amends. Once this happens and behaviour change occurs over time, trust will be rebuilt and emotional connection will begin to develop once again.

Be patient. It may take time to rebuild trust, depending on the nature of the offence. The offending party should be willing to make a 'living amends' which is similar to the 'living sacrifice' called for in Scripture (Romans 12:1–2). That is, a lifestyle change that they are committed to regardless of whether anyone forgives them or reconciles with them. This will signal to others that they have truly experienced a change in their values, thoughts and beliefs. This sort of changed person is likely to rebuild trust over time – not demanding it, but humbly seeking it.

WRITE AND REFLECT

When, if ever, have you experienced a reconciled relationship where the offended party forgave, and the offending party made a complete amends (all five parts)? What was that process like for you?

UNRECONCILED RELATIONSHIPS

Scenario #1: The offended party has forgiven, but the offending party will not make amends.

Alexa

As far as my dad goes, God gave me so much grace. I forgave my dad. I felt led to write him a letter about four years ago. I told him how much I loved him and wondered if he could write me a letter and let me know how he felt about me. I knew it would do more harm than good to tell him how his lack of showing his love for me hurt. In his mind he did love us kids and should not be asked to say it. His health was rather poor, and I needed to do this. I knew I was taking a big risk of once more being rejected but I decided I would have no expectations and trust God whatever the outcome. I would like to tell you that he just melted and told me everything I had always wanted to hear, but he did not. In fact, it made him mad. But I had no expectations, so I wasn't crushed. No, he could not tell me those things. But I noticed after that, he began telling all four of us kids that he loved us every time we were with him. God did soften his heart towards himself and all of the family. We became closer before Alzheimer's took his memory and then his life, and God allowed me to be by his side as he died. I got to tell him everything I wanted to before he went to heaven. Thank you, God.

When we have forgiven someone, but they have not made amends – perhaps do not even realize they have offended us or owe us an amends – what should we do?

There are essentially two options, listed below. You will note that unforgiveness is not listed as an option. That is because the physical, mental and emotional benefits of forgiveness are well-documented in both biblical and extra-biblical sources. So, while technically unforgiveness is an option, it is not a healthy one as it encourages the offended party to harbour bitterness and anger. Moreover, usually unforgiveness is given as an option to protect the offended party from further harm. This is *not* necessary. It *is* possible to forgive *and* set limits that insulate the offended party from further harm.

Reconciliation is also not listed as an option. That is because reconciliation cannot occur unless there is both forgiveness and amends.

All that said, I consider there to be two viable options for people who have been hurt by someone who is not repentant or has not made a complete amends.[34]

The first is to *forgive and not to interact* – this may be a good option when the offending party has not made amends, is likely to harm you again and there is no need for you to be around them. You can still gain the benefits of forgiveness without being in relationship with this person.

The second is to *forgive and interact* – this may be a good option when the offending party has not made amends, or they have made amends but trust has not yet been rebuilt and they are someone who you want to be around or have no choice but to be around. It might be a co-worker or family member that you cannot avoid, or do not want to fully break relationship with. In this case, although you may have or want to interact with them, you do not have to make yourself emotionally or physically vulnerable to them. Do not share feelings and avoid being alone with them.

34 Suzanne Freedman, 'Forgiveness and Reconciliation: The Importance of Understanding How They Differ', *Counseling and Values*, vol 42 (3), (1998), pp. 200-216.

Whether it is appropriate to either interact or not interact given the situation, you might also find it helpful to do the following:

- Pray for them to recognize their need to make amends.
- Love them (from a distance).
- Remember your value is in Christ, not in their opinion of you.
- Maintain your boundaries and limits with this person.
- Do not enable destructive behaviour – allow them to experience the consequences of their behaviour.
- Trust in God's timing – he has them in a change process and his will is working its way out in their life.

WRITE AND REFLECT

Which of the above options seem appropriate to you concerning your relationship with people who have hurt you but have not been willing to make a complete amends, and why?

UNRECONCILED RELATIONSHIPS

Scenario #2: The offending party has made amends, but the offended party won't forgive.

Deanna

It was very important for me to come to process and talk through those feelings in safe community each week. It enabled me to keep my commitment and transform my parenting. It took four months for my oldest daughter to take small steps towards trusting me again, and seven months before we could truly connect. It has been a long and difficult process, but it has been so worth the struggle.

If there is someone we hurt, and we have made a complete amends to them but they have not forgiven us, what should we do?

This is a difficult situation, as we may sincerely desire reconciliation. However, no matter how much we want it to happen, we cannot force someone to forgive us. In fact, the more pressure we put on the person to forgive, the more likely we are to re-injure them by imposing our will on them. Do not demand forgiveness or manipulate with biblical commands to forgive.

It is possible that the person we have harmed will sense that they have us at a disadvantage and may begin placing demands on us that violate our values. We may be tempted to give in to these demands to win back the relationship. This may relieve the tension in the relationship in the short term. However, in the long term we may begin to feel resentful towards the person we harmed for pressuring us to violate our values, which will only further complicate the reconciliation process. It is better to maintain our integrity and boundaries while searching for ways to compromise or negotiate a solution that works for both those involved, for example, using the IPA WIN strategy discussed in Chapter 10.

We can also continue to love them, even if from a distance.

We can pray for them and be kind to them. We can gently express hope that they will forgive us, while also letting them know that we understand and accept that it may take some time for them to forgive.

If the person we hope will forgive us is a follower of Christ, we have a unique asset. Jesus is a minister of reconciliation, and he urges those who follow him to forgive as they were forgiven. And he promises that he will continue the good work that he began in us, shaping us more and more into his likeness. Based on these promises, we have good reason to trust God to convict the person of their unforgiveness in his timing.

While you wait on God's timing, I urge you to continue working on your own change process. Do not wait to change until you are forgiven. Do it for you, so that you can be the person God is calling you to be – regardless of the status of the damaged relationship. This is your living amends towards the person you hurt, and your living sacrifice to the God who long ago forgave and redeemed you.

Continue to empathize with the hurt of the offended person if they open up to you and share how they are feeling. Be prepared for them to say some things that may be difficult to hear as they tell you how they have been hurt. Remember your value is in Christ, not in their opinion of you or in your past mistakes.

Even if it takes more time than you would like for reconciliation to happen, you can rest knowing that if you have done all of the above, you are doing what you can to restore the relationship as far as it depends on you. Your 'side of the street' will be clean, and that is all anyone can ask of you.

Malik

I struggled with forgiveness and realizing that I was forgiven. I had been working so hard, chasing after God with all my heart. I had been diligent and working through biblical principles that would help bring about change in my life. Eventually, I realized that God had forgiven me and I had forgiven myself when my old wrongdoings were brought up during an argument and the typical feelings of guilt, shame and defeat did not come upon me like they usually did. I realized that, although I had done those things, they didn't define me for who I am. I do not see myself as that man anymore. I was surprised and relieved to realize the benefits of God's forgiveness, and my forgiveness of myself, in such a tangible way right then in that moment.

My favourite Scripture from my Step Study is Isaiah 1:18:

> 'Come now, let us settle the matter,'
>   says the LORD.
> 'Though your sins are like scarlet,
>   they shall be as white as snow;
> though they are red as crimson,
>   they shall be like wool.' NIV

I felt no more guilt. The man of the past was dead, his sins were washed clean, and he is now new and forgiven.

WRITE AND REFLECT

What experiences have you had in making amends with someone who would not forgive you, or with whom you have been unable to reconcile? What next steps are you feeling led to take?

CHAPTER 13

MISSIONAL VISION

… you are not fit to build and lead a team until you've worked hard on yourself.

KOUZES AND POSNER[35]

Everything can be taken from a man but one thing: the last of the human freedoms – to choose one's attitude in any given set of circumstances, to choose one's own way.

VIKTOR E. FRANKL, HOLOCAUST SURVIVOR AND CREATOR OF LOGOTHERAPY

'You are the light of the world. A city located on a hill cannot be hidden. People do not light a lamp and put it under a basket but on a lampstand, and it gives light to all in the house. In the same way, let your light shine before people, so that they can see your good deeds and give honor to your Father in heaven.'

MATTHEW 5:14-16

YOUR PURPOSE, MISSION AND VISION

By now you have gained a greater understanding of your past and how it has affected you. This will shed light on why you believe and think as you do. It will have helped you to discover why you are

---

35 James M. Kouzes, Barry Z. Posner, *The Leadership Challenge: How to Make Extraordinary Things Happen in Organizations* (John Wiley & Sons, 2017) p.52.

passionate about a specific cause, why your values are what they are and where your faith fits into this. You may have learned, for example, that the pain and difficulty of your past has constituted you in a specific way, but that whatever marks it has left on you can be seen not as disqualifying you from service, but rather as qualifications for service to people with the same kinds of struggles that you yourself have lived through (2 Corinthians 1:3–5).

This process has been essential, because understanding our values and their source is what gives us the courage of conviction to stand by them in difficult times, and to lead others by inspiring them to connect with their own values. This is not to say that the source of our values is only our lived experience, and that these values are not God-given.

It is our experiences, plus the way God made us, plus his word, his people and his Spirit, all swirling around together, that have created the longings for justice or mercy or beauty (or whatever we long for).

And by going through this process, you will have also become entangled with different strategies, people and skills that will help you to maintain healthy thoughts, manage destructive emotions and create strategies to deal with behavioural and relational difficulties. These skills are also essential to staying healthy and maintaining your character as you develop skills, realize your goals and expand your influence. My hope is that this book may have been for you a sort of beaker, into which the various experiences, information and people networks that have shaped you have been poured and heated, creating a combustible reaction that will propel you forward into your life's purpose and mission.

Pursuit of purpose helps to build joy and meaning into life. This explains why Rick Warren's book, *40 Days of Purpose*,[36] has sold over 30 million copies since it was published in 2002.

It explains why Jewish psychologist Viktor Frankl, whilst he

---

36 Rick Warren, *40 Days of Purpose* (Purpose Driven Ministries, 2003).

suffered in a Nazi death camp, arrived at the conclusion that a sense of purpose is what gives value to life, and that when it is lost there's nothing left to live for. He created Logotherapy after he was liberated, which is centred around the concept that mental health has everything to do with finding meaning in life through purpose.

It explains why positive psychology research has determined that one of the seven essential qualities of a happy life is 'transcendent purpose'.

It explains why treatment for those suffering from borderline personality disorder involves the skill of identifying personal values and translating them into action steps.

It explains why Motivational Interviewing techniques, developed for use with people struggling with addiction, help people identify what they care about, and then heighten the discrepancy between their goals and their current behaviour. The hope is that the desire to achieve life goals works like a winch to pull the person out of addiction, and into values-directed behaviour.

The bottom line is that joyful pursuit – not attainment – of a transcendent purpose seems to be at least half the point of a fulfilling life. Solomon wrote:

> *There is nothing better for people than to eat and drink,*
> *and to find enjoyment in their work.*
> *I also perceived that this ability to find enjoyment comes*
> *from God.*

ECCLESIASTES 2:24

When you think about it, that's a relief, since the majority of our time is spent in pursuit of life goals, rather than in their attainment.

REFINING YOUR LIFE GOALS

The following exercise is to help you refine your life goals by factoring in whatever has been brought to light for you as you've worked through this book. You can also use this information to draw from as you figure out how to communicate your vision to others who can somehow contribute to your cause.

We will start with the **Why**, then get to **What,** and then the **How** it is that you actually want to act on your values. This exercise will help you to articulate to others *why* they should care about what you care about before they decide whether to pay any attention to *what* you are saying you want to do, or *how* you are going to go about doing it.

And if, as you begin writing, it seems that you are dreaming of something too big – too audacious – to even tell anyone else what you are considering, then that means you are on the right track! God is not interested in plans that we can do ourselves. He is interested in plans so big that they can only be accomplished if he is right in the middle of them. So, make your dreams bigger than anything you could ever achieve on your own. Remember, 'I am able to do all things through the one who strengthens me' (Philippians 4:13) and 'He who calls you is trustworthy, and he will in fact do this' (1 Thessalonians 5:24).

MY MISSIONAL VISION

Why

Why do you want to address this issue, or achieve this goal?

What is it about your own personal story or experiences that inspires you?

Why might others connect to your vision, and be inspired to care about what you care about?

How does Scripture speak to this issue?

What

What is your vision, or dream, for how this will look if you are successful?

How

How can you join with people who are already doing this?

If there is a need to chase this vision in a way that is different or better than what others are doing, how will you do it differently or better?

How will you use the skills and gifts you already have to help you to do this?

What other training will you need and how will it help you?

What people will help?

What other resources will you use?

The Ask

Drawing from everything that you wrote about in the three sections above, write a script that communicates your vision to someone who can make a contribution of time, talent or treasure to your cause. Be passionate. Use emotion. Tell your story, and why this is so important to you.

EPILOGUE: MOVING FORWARD

For every high priest is taken from among the people and appointed to represent them before God, to offer both gifts and sacrifices for sins. He is able to deal compassionately with those who are ignorant and erring, since he also is subject to weakness … During his earthly life Christ offered both requests and supplications, with loud cries and tears, to the one who was able to save him from death and he was heard because of his devotion. Although he was a son, he learned obedience through the things he suffered. And by being perfected in this way, he became the source of eternal salvation to all who obey him, and he was designated by God as high priest in the order of Melchizedek.

HEBREWS 5:1–2, 7–10

Jesus was a better high priest than any other. Why? Because he was perfectly obedient, yet suffered unjustly, even to the point of death. He understands abandonment, hatred, rejection, slander, imprisonment, grief, abuse of every kind, hunger, thirst, having goals blocked by others, betrayal, alienation – all of it. He understands the worst kind of temptation. He has experienced the maximum level of pain through many experiences. And so, when we bring our struggles to him, he gets it because he went through it, or something like it, himself.

You've gone through it, too. Whatever denial you were in, whatever was left unexplored, whatever you kept hidden or simply didn't have occasion to write down or bring into the light of relationship with others, it's all part of your ongoing story. You know what it is to feel vulnerable with another person, and God. To risk rejection or judgment but receive grace.

So when others share their story or struggles with you, you'll get it – just like Jesus. It doesn't matter if you haven't experienced the exact same kinds of struggles others have experienced – the point is that you know what it is like to struggle, so you can relate. And on top of that, you now have an expansive set of new tools that might help others with their thoughts, feelings or behaviours. You learned how to use them by applying them to your own life.

Through this process, you've discovered what has shaped you: the things that happened, or didn't happen, that made and unmade you. From this review of your life, you've gained insight into the values you hold, where they come from and why they are so meaningful for you. And from these experiences, these struggles, you've built a missional vision that will help you live out your values. You can pursue and achieve the purpose for which you've been made.

My encouragement to you now is to go do it. Whatever it is for you. Move forward. If someone is already doing it, join their team. If no one is doing it, or they're not doing it quite the way you would, then go start something new. Let your passion fuel your vision. Draw from the experiences that formed you, the people in your sphere of influence and the resources at your disposal. God uses everything. Nothing is wasted. He weaves it all together. By faith, choose to believe that the God who made you, who allowed in your life what he allowed – didn't cause it to happen but allowed it for a reason – and that he is going to see you through it.

As you live out your passion, remember your tools. Attend to your thoughts, build some joy into your life, maintain community, act against destructive emotions. Attend to your relationships – don't get weighed down by unforgiveness, guilt or shame. Instead, forgive, set limits when you need to and promptly make amends when you violate your own values.

Don't fool yourself into thinking you can sweep things under the rug. Remember, there is no rug. That's just a metaphor. Your entanglements matter, so watch what you become entangled with.

When life gets thick, remember you have an ally who you can meet with when you need to – here on earth in the form of a friend you can trust, and in the form of a Supreme Ally in heaven, through Christ. And remember to be an ally for someone else along the way, whether in your workplace, school, family, neighbourhood, at the café, at church or wherever. There's no one else like you. You were made for great things such as this.

I pray that you will remain attuned to the tangible presence of the God of heaven and earth who created you, loves you and walks with you each and every day. Never stop speaking to him, listening to him, reading his word, meeting with his people and noticing the expressions of his love in your life.

God bless you.

Forward! He is your Foundation!

APPENDIX 1

The following is a list of resources for those who would like to explore the Christian faith further.

ON THE WEB

www.rzim.org – Lists multiple web-based resources on apologetics.

www.gotquestions.org – For questions about God, Jesus and the Bible.

www.netbible.org – An online Bible, well-referenced translation notes and study notes, as well as a separate set of notes by theologian Dr Thomas L. Constable.

www.intelligentdesign.org – For ongoing scientific discussion of the rational argument for the existence of God based on the design of the universe.

www.exploregod.com – A compilation of resources for those interested in exploring the concept of a biblical, personal God who loves them.

www.iamsecond.com – Collection of video testimonies from people, many of whom are celebrities, whose lives have been transformed by the love of Christ.

www.truthforlife.org - Topical teaching from an experienced pastor.

voice.dts.edu/chapel - A large collection of teachings on a variety of topics from a well-respected seminary in Dallas, Texas.

BOOKS

The following is another very brief list, but it is enough to begin exploring God's existence and attributes.

The Purpose Driven Life Rick Warren

Life Without Limits Nick Vujicic

Mere Christianity C.S. Lewis

Crazy Love Francis Chan

The Reason for God Timothy Keller

What's So Great About Christianity Dinesh D'Souza

What's So Amazing About Grace Philip Yancey

Seeking Allah Finding Jesus Nabeel Qureshi

The Shack William P. Young

More than a Carpenter Josh McDowell

The Case for Christ Lee Strobel

APPENDIX 2

There are many forms of care that, one way or another, tap into the feature of our brains that allows us to change the way we act and feel by changing the way we think.[37] Indeed, by changing the way we think, we change the material structure of our brain itself.

This concept is called 'Neural Plasticity'. This means that our brains aren't fixed organs that do not change. Instead, they are affected by our experiences – shaped by what happens to us, what we do and how we think. That quality enables us to strengthen or change our neural connections, according to researchers.[38]

This is good news. It means that when it comes to how we think, feel and act, we are not just passive bystanders. There are always going to be things in life that we don't like and cannot change, but we can change the way that we choose to think about them. We can find ways to turn negatives into positives, look on the bright side, put things into perspective or make lemonade out of lemons. We can choose to think in ways that support us in becoming the people we are called to be. And ultimately, because of neural plasticity, we can change the actual physical structure of our brain by changing our mind.

Another significant feature of our brain that helps us to

37 Cognitive Behavioral Therapy (CBT), Neuro-Linguistic Programming (NLP), Dialectical Behavior Therapy (DBT), Eye Movement Desensitization and Reprocessing (EMDR) and Rational Emotive Behavioral Therapy (REBT) are examples of therapeutic modalities that, in one way or another, help clients identify and modify thoughts to effect behavioral, emotional and physiological changes.

38 Paquette, V., Lévesque, J., Mensour, B., Leroux, J., Beaudoin, G., Bourgouin, P., Beauregard, M., '"Change the mind and you change the brain": Effects of cognitive-behavioral therapy on the neural correlates of spider phobia' in *NeuroImage*, 18, vol. 2 (2003), pp. 401-9.

change the way we think about difficult experiences is called the Reticular Activation System (RAS). Neuropsychologists tell us that this is the part of the brain that is responsible for helping us focus on things that are important – that is, goal directed activity.[39] Practitioners of Neuro Linguistic Programming (NLP)[40] argue that the RAS is involved in bringing into our conscious awareness the things around us that are related to our goals. The idea is that, once we set a goal, we begin noticing resources in our environment that will help us become more likely to achieve that goal. The RAS also filters out information that creates obstacles to our goal.

If you would like to read more about the research behind these concepts, or the kinds of therapies that were designed with these features of our brain in mind, the references at the bottom of the previous page will get you started.

---

39 Kinomura, S., Larsson, J., Gulyás, B., Roland, P. 'Activation by Attention of the Human Reticular Formation and Thalamic Intralaminar Nuclei', in *Science*, vol. 271, (1996), pp. 512-515.
40 Robbins, A., *Awaken the Giant Within* (Fireside, 1992).

God doesn't give us answers. In the silence he gives us himself - bigger than our pain, beyond our explanations, closer than our breath.

ALAIN EMERSON

When you follow God in wholehearted obedience, and suddenly your entire world falls apart; when your deepest, most urgent prayers are met with silence – can faith survive?

Alain Emerson felt like the luckiest man in the world. The talented pastor of a thriving church and national director of a prayer movement, he had found and married Lindsay, his soulmate. He could never have imagined that in a matter of months he would be nursing his twenty-three-year-old wife through the final stages of cancer, and would find himself as a young widower, distraught and alone.

In Luminous Dark Alain retraces his journey through the stages of grief, pain and shock, choosing to lean into the pain and to face God with his disappointment in the dark tunnel of despair. It is here that Alain wrestles with God and with his grief.

And it is from that he emerges with a sense of having seen God's face – the one who knows our pain, who walks beside us, suffers and weeps with us, and who ultimately restores our joy.

Luminous Dark
Alain Emerson
ISBN: 978-1-910012-45-1
Price: £12.99

Muddy
Pearl

A beautifully written book that reflects both a tender heart and a lucid mind ... like water in the desert, it will provide you with a refreshing perspective on illness and suffering.

PABLO MARTINEZ

'When I fell ill and stayed ill, I felt like God had chopped me off at the ankles. I yelped in pain and indignation, I felt painfully abandoned, diminished and finished. It took me a long time to learn that God was not out to kill me.'

Some illnesses begin with a bang, whipped off to hospital or flattened into bed. Other conditions creep in until normal life is no longer normal. Life skills are suddenly out of date. Work, socialising and hobbies are out of reach. It's a new and scary world.

Emily Ackerman knows this world only too well. She knows what it feels like to cry out to God to relieve her suffering, to allow her to fulfil her life plans. She knows what it feels like to wait, year after year, while God works through her suffering, to fulfil his plans for her life.

This book is about fighting back. It's about reclaiming your life now you're ill, and finding new ways to live well and serve effectively. You'll find survival strategies, encouragement, practical advice and fresh ways to view your situation. God hasn't given up on you: there's good news from the Bible about living abundantly and usefully with illness.

The Amazing Technicolour Pyjama Therapy
Emily Ackerman
ISBN: 978-1-910012-12-3
Price: £9.99

Muddy
Pearl